Popular Culture and the Political Values of Neoliberalism

Politics, Literature, and Film

Series Editor: Lee Trepanier, Saginaw Valley State University

The Politics, Literature Film series is an interdisciplinary examination of the intersection of politics with literature and/or film. The series is receptive to works that use a variety of methodological approaches, focus on any period from antiquity to the present, and situate their analysis in national, comparative, or global contexts. Politics, Literature, and Film seeks to be truly interdisciplinary by including authors from all the social sciences and humanities, such as political science, sociology, psychology, literature, philosophy, history, religious studies, and law. The series is open to both American and non-American literature and film. By putting forth bold and innovative ideas that appeal to a broad range of interests, the series aims to enrich our conver-sations about literature, film, and their relationship to politics.

Advisory Board

Richard Avaramenko, University of Wisconsin-Madison
Linda Beail, Point Loma Nazarene University
Claudia Franziska Brühwiler, University of St. Gallen
Timothy Burns, Baylor University
Paul A. Cantor, University of Virginia
Joshua Foa Dienstag, University of California at Los Angeles
Lilly Goren, Carroll University
Natalie Taylor, Skidmore College
Ann Ward, University of Regina
Catherine Heldt Zuckert, University of Notre Dame

Recent Titles

Milton's Socratic Rationalism: The Conversations of Adam and Eve in Paradise Lost, by David Oliver Davies
Walker Percy and the Politics of the Wayfarer, by Brian A. Smith
Romanticism and Civilization: Love, Marriage and Family in Rousseau's Julie, by Mark Kremer
Aldous Huxley: The Political Thought of a Man of Letters, by Alessandro Maurini
Sinclair Lewis and American Democracy, by Steven Michels
Liberty, Individuality, and Democracy in Jorge Luis Borges, by Alejandra M. Salinas
Philip Roth and American Liberalism: Historical Content and Literary Form in the Later Works, by Andy Connolly
Seeing through the Screen: Interpreting American Political Film, by Bruce E. Altschuler
Cowboy Politics: Myths and Discourses in Popular Westerns from The Virginian *to* Unforgiven *and* Deadwood, by John S. Nelson
Beyond Free Speech and Propaganda: The Political Development of Hollywood, 1907–1927, by John D. Steinmetz

Politics, Hollywood Style: American Politics in Film from Mr. Smith to Selma, by John Heyrman
Civil Servants on the Silver Screen: Hollywood's Depiction of Government and Bureaucrats, by Michelle C. Pautz
The Pursuit of Happiness and the American Regime: Political Theory in Literature, by Elizabeth Amato
Imagination and Environmental Political Thought: The Aftermath of Thoreau, by Joshua J. Bowman
The American Road Trip and American Political Thought, by Susan McWilliams Barndt
Flattering the Demos: Fiction and Democratic Education, by Travis Smith and Marlene Sokolon
Soul of Statesmanship: Shakespeare on Nature, Virtue, and Political Wisdom, by Khalil M. Habib and L. Joseph Hebert Jr.
Part of Our National Culture: Part of Our National Culture, by Eric Kasper and Quentin Vieregge
Short Stories and Political Philosophy: Power, Prose, and Persuasion, by Erin A. Dolgoy, Kimberly Hurd Hale, and Bruce Peabody
Human Nature and Politics in Utopian and Anti-Utopian Fiction, by Nivedita Bagchi
Wonder and Cruelty: Ontological War in "It's a Wonderful Life," by Steven Johnston
Rabelais's Contempt for Fortune: Pantagruelism, Politics, and Philosophy, by Timothy Haglund
The Coen Brothers and the Comedy of Democracy, by Barry Craig and Sara MacDonald
Popular Culture and the Political Values of Neoliberalism, by George A. Gonzalez

Popular Culture and the Political Values of Neoliberalism

George A. Gonzalez

LEXINGTON BOOKS
Lanham • Boulder • New York • London

Published by Lexington Books
An imprint of The Rowman & Littlefield Publishing Group, Inc.
4501 Forbes Boulevard, Suite 200, Lanham, Maryland 20706
www.rowman.com

6 Tinworth Street, London SE11 5AL, United Kingdom

Copyright © 2019 by The Rowman & Littlefield Publishing Group, Inc.

All rights reserved. No part of this book may be reproduced in any form or by any electronic or mechanical means, including information storage and retrieval systems, without written permission from the publisher, except by a reviewer who may quote passages in a review.

British Library Cataloguing in Publication Information Available

Library of Congress Cataloging-in-Publication Data Available

ISBN 978-1-4985-9185-0 (cloth)
ISBN 978-1-4985-9187-4 (pbk)
ISBN 978-1-4985-9186-7 (electronic)

For Ileana and Alana

Contents

Introduction		1
1	Capitalism and the Absolute	5
2	Analytic Philosophy and Star Trek	19
3	Abraham Lincoln as Globalist	27
4	The Politics of Race and Class Oppression in Star Trek	41
5	Popular Culture on Good, Evil, and Post-Traumatic Stress Disorder	51
6	Clones and the Politics of the Mind in Star Wars and Star Trek	59
7	Art as Knowledge: Who Leads the American World System	67
8	Popular Culture and Trump Politics	79
Conclusion: Popular Culture and Reasons in the World		91
Bibliography		95
Index		105
About the Author		109

Introduction

Reality is made up of the *Absolute* and causality. The *absolute* (most saliently philosophized about by Georg Hegel) is where normative values inhere. Causality can be described as the measurable effects of the normative values of the absolute and the laws of physics (also ostensibly a product of the absolute). Humans are special insofar as they access the *higher* aspects of the Absolute—altruism, compassion, love, humor, science, engineering, and so on. The Absolute also contains what can be considered the less attractive values or impulses: greed, lust for power, hate, self-centeredness, conceit, and so on (chapter 2). Predicating society on what I deem the lower (*spirits*) aspects of the absolute (most prominently, *greed*) results in personal, social dysfunction and ultimately the end of civilization. Conversely, a society based on *justice* is stable and vibrant. Justice is a classless society, free of gender and ethnic biases. My argument is based on popular culture—especially the Star Trek franchise. One implication of my thesis is that capitalist values generate psychological neurosis and societal instability—even catastrophe (chapter 1) Additionally, the political values that dominate the current *neoliberalist* world system (and especially the American government) are *the other* (chapters 3 and 4), the *will to power* (chapter 8)—resulting in war (chapters 5 and 6), and global political instability (chapter 7).

ART AS KNOWLEDGE

Classicist Henry Paolucci explains that "art" (along with religion and philosophy) "are in the end, for Hegel, 'moments' of *absolute spirit*."[1] Similarly, philosopher William Desmond, in *A Study of Hegel's Aesthetics: Art and the Absolute*, notes that "[a]rt has an *absolute* dimension; indeed, it belongs together with religion and philosophy itself as one of the three highest modes of human meaning."[2] Consonant with Hegelian reasoning, my specific argument in this volume is that the broadcast iterations of Star Trek allow us to comprehend significant aspects of the absolute—particularly as it relates to justice. Therefore, Star Trek is the highest of high-brow entertainment.[3] Why is art empirical documentation of the *absolute*?[4] Humans speculate about the absolute—that is, that which moves history forward and allows people to lead authentic lives. Precisely because the *absolute* is that which is and which isn't,[5] art/imagination allows for the *absolute* to be conveyed in an intellectually and emotionally satisfying matter.[6] (Notably, the first known philosophy in the Western world [Plato's *Dialogues*] was written in the form of narrative art.) Art, therefore, can supersede philosophy, with the latter serving to dissect/amplify what is accessed/depicted through the former.

A simple but nonetheless informative example being the *Next Generation* episode "All Goods Things . . . " (1994). The "little pond of goo" from which all life on Earth emanated is conveyed. It is from this *pond of goo* that the *absolute* for organic life on Earth was born, as here is where the will (i.e., *spirit*) to live/survive/procreate on this planet was spawned. Star Trek aptly notes that the destruction of this pond, and all like it, would have prevented humans from evolving. It is through such portrayals that we can *see* how the absolute operates with regard to life on Earth (of course, including humans).

The enduring popularity of Star Trek indicates the validity of the speculation portrayed in the franchise about the absolute. Put differently, the global success of the Star Trek text validates the idea that the multiple series and movies, to an important degree, "capture" the essence of the absolute. Philosophy professor Jack Kaminsky, drawing explicitly on Hegel's theory of aesthetics, explains that "the artist tries to show men what kind of man would be the fullest expression of the Idea" (i.e., the Absolute).[7] Therefore, very plausibly, the artistic success of the Star Trek franchise (and its great popularity) is precisely due to the fact that it shows us *what kind of person/society would be the fullest expression of the Absolute*. Precisely because of Star Trek we can seemingly be secure about certain aspects of the absolute, and, as a result, Star Trek ostensibly serves as a guide to an authentic life and a stable, thriving society. Parenthetically, the value of Star Trek is exactly that it transcends the personalities and specific contexts within which it was produced. Indeed, this is precisely what makes it effective, elucidating political theory and philosophy.

Analytic philosophy, whose adherents have historically ridiculed the idea of the absolute[8]—without positing any answers of their own for the movement of history[9]—is an obstacle to knowledge. Most specifically, art and the analyzing of the aesthetic are viewed by analytic philosophers as mainly outside of epistemology and ignorable as it relates to science.[10] The humanities is of a piece with the physical sciences[11]—as they both *speculate* about the absolute, the latter about its manifestation in matter and energy, whereas the former (in its finer forms) is *speculation* about the absolute as it pertains to human affairs.[12] "Art may not have the precision of physics but, according to Hegel, it has as crucial a role in revealing to us an aspect of the [Absolute] Idea."[13] Because analytic philosophers reject the arts as a source of knowledge, this approach serves to block the truth—knowledge of the absolute through art. Star Trek is directly predicated on Hegelian reasoning about the *Absolute* (chapter 2).

OVERVIEW OF BOOK

Looking to art (specifically Star Trek), we can observe the personal and social perniciousness of greed. Greed, within a capitalist/neoliberalist context, functions as a destructive addiction and results in social catastrophe (chapter 1). Chapters 3 and 4 take up the issue of identity politics. Star Trek indicates that the only *authentic* identity is that of globalism—whereby all humans are citizens of the world (expressly rejecting the politics of *the other*). Chapters 5 and 6 are about the *mind*. The condition of *post-traumatic stress disorder* (PTSD) is proof positive that the human mind is geared toward forwarding the progressive dialectic, and direct, violent (murderous) acts against this dialectic (e.g., imperial war) literally damages the mind (chapter 5). Both Star Wars and Star Trek posit the literary device of (warrior) clones. Examining these literary devices allows us to conclude that the mind inherently has an autonomous relationship to the Absolute (chapter 6). With chapter 7, I change gears somewhat and focus specifically on U.S. politics. In addition to Star Trek, I engage the television series *Justice League Unlimited*, *The Blacklist*, and *House of Cards* to show that the American government (under the auspices of neoliberalism) has become decisively authoritarian. The final chapter (chapter 8) treats the destructive political values underlying the series *Breaking Bad*. These political values are those of neoliberalism and propelled the rise of Donald Trump. The corrosive political values of neoliberalism are juxtaposed to a politics based on solidarity as cast in the Star Trek franchise.

NOTES

1. Henry Paolucci, "Introduction," in *Hegel: On the Arts*, Henry Paolucci, ed., second edition (Smyrna, DE: Griffon House, 2001), xix, emphasis added.
2. William Desmond, *Art and the Absolute: A Study of Hegel's Aesthetics* (Albany: State University of New York Press, 1986), xii, emphasis added.
3. Lawrence Levine, *Highbrow/Lowbrow: The Emergence of Cultural Hierarchy in America* (Cambridge, MA: Harvard University Press, 1990); Jason T. Eberl and Kevin S. Decker, eds., *Star Trek and Philosophy: The Wrath of Khan* (Chicago: Open Court, 2008).
4. Jack Kaminsky, *Hegel on Art: An Interpretation of Hegel's Aesthetics* (Albany: State University of New York Press, 1962).

5. Stephen Mumford, *Metaphysics: A Very Short Introduction* (New York: New York: Oxford University Press, 2012).

6. Richard Eldridge, *Beyond Representation: Philosophy and Poetic Imagination* (New York: Cambridge University Press, 2011); Jennifer Ann Bates, *Hegel's Theory of Imagination* (Albany: State University of New York Press, 2004).

7. Kaminsky, *Hegel on Art*, 29.

8. Hans-Johann Glock, *What Is Analytic Philosophy?* (New York: Cambridge University Press, 2008), 117–21.

9. Ibid., chap. 4.

10. Jan Westerhoff, *Reality: A Very Short Introduction* (New York: Oxford University Press, 2012).

11. Siân Ede, *Art and Science* (New York: I. B. Tauris, 2005); Martin Kemp, *Seen | Unseen: Art, Science, and Intuition from Leonardo to the Hubble Telescope* (New York: Oxford University Press, 2006); Steven Connor, "Doing without Art," *New Literary History* 42, no. 1: 53–69; Bence Nanay, *Aesthetics as Philosophy of Perception* (New York: Oxford University Press, 2016).

12. For example, Rebecca Solnit, "Bird by Bird," *New York Times Magazine*, December 7, 2014, MM13; Adam Frank, "Is a Climate Disaster Inevitable?" *New York Times*, January 18, 2015, SR6.

13. Kaminsky, *Hegel on Art*, 21.

Chapter One

Capitalism and the Absolute

The creators of Star Wars are essentially correct about the *Force* (i.e., the absolute): there is a *Dark Side* and a *Good Side*. At the risk of being impolitic, capitalism is predicated on the Dark Side of the absolute. Adam Smith famously argued that individual self-interest (defined as personal material acquisitiveness) is the basis of economic progress.[1] The character Gordon Gekko in the 1987 movie *Wall Street* put it most stridently when he argued that "[g]reed, for lack of a better word, is good." Gekko went on to explain that "[g]reed, in all of its forms . . . greed for life, for money, for love, knowledge . . . has marked the upward surge of mankind." Closer to Smith's argument and ethos, the character Quark (a Ferengi) from the Star Trek series *Deep Space Nine* held that "Greed is the purest . . . of emotions. . . . Greed is Eternal."[2] Thus, while Smith would seemingly not agree that greed in all spheres of life is appropriate, his argument was that greed (individual material acquisitiveness) was the only (or minimally the most) reliable emotion to base a global economy upon.

Certainly, many emotions, motives are the basis of modernity and the modern global economy—for example, democracy, new knowledge (technology), adventure, the desire for interesting work. (It's no accident that the modern global economy embedded and expanded the Enlightenment.) Additionally, Smith did acknowledge that there may be times when the profit motive does not serve the community, nation and in those instances should be curbed. The Russian Revolution of 1917 was a reaction against the profit motive as a guiding social principle. The Great Depression in the 1930s also prompted even in the advanced capitalist world sustained efforts to check and regulate the greed underlying the profit motive (e.g., the U.S. New Deal).[3]

Gekko's famous lines and Quark's vaunting of greed are reflective of the politics of neoliberalism. Gekko's defense of greed is made as part of his proposal to dismantle a unionized work force in order to maximize shareholder profit. Such an assault on unions and unionized work were hallmarks of American economy in the 1980s and the 1990s, as the New Deal ended with the election of Ronald Reagan in 1980 and the accompanying Reagan Revolution.[4] The Reagan Revolution accelerated the process where the profit motive (greed) became the highest political value for the United States and (for the first time in human history) the entire world (in other words, *global neoliberalism*). This extended to the formerly state socialist societies of China and the Soviet Union (now Russia and other new nation-states carved out of what was the Soviet Union). Neoliberalism is the idea that capital, goods, and services should be allowed to find their most profitable outlets—on a worldwide scale. Hence, what profoundly, decisively shapes the world economy today is the quest for profit and profit-maximizing (i.e., greed).[5] In the case of Quark, he asserted the superiority of greed as a social force in response to an effort to shift Ferengi values to a foundation of "benevolence"—altruism, charity. Before I further develop my arguments concerning the Absolute and its relation to capitalism, I will engage the school of thought that denies the very existence of the absolute: *analytic philosophy*.

POLITICAL THEORY AND ANALYTIC PHILOSOPHY

Proponents of analytic philosophy hold that only the (measurable) world of causality is real, actual. The absolute, according to analytic philosophers, simply does not exist.[6] On its face, this position is illogical. Analytic philosophers hold that their philosophical approach is an adjunct to the physical sciences. Nevertheless, the prime object of study of the physical sciences is the laws of physics—that which determines the behavior of matter and energy. The laws of physics cannot be directly observed. What the sciences do is measure the response of matter and energy to the laws but not the laws themselves. We cannot see, touch, or measure the laws of gravity, conservation, thermal dynamics, and so on. We understand the ontology of these so-called laws, and nothing else. Similarly, we can only comprehend the ontology of greed, love, altruism, compassion, power lust, and so forth. Most broadly, we're limited to seeing the ontology of the Absolute, and cannot analyze it as a *thing*. Therefore, we can study the effects of greed or gravity (for instance), but not greed nor gravity itself.

Closely related to analytic philosophy are *pragmatism* and *neo-pragmatism*.[7] Georg Hegel—who most saliently philosophized about the absolute—held that *justice* inheres in the absolute. With analytic philosophers limiting themselves to what they can physically sense, they deny the existence of justice as a metaphysical entity. Pragmatism and neo-pragmatism come closest to being the political philosophy of analytic philosophy. This is because their authors deny that justice exists. For pragmatists, who originated from the nineteenth-century American scene, the highest political value is *stability*. Harvard historian Louis Menand points out that the core of pragmatism is "the belief that ideas [ethics, morality] should never become ideologies"—which early pragmatists saw as the cause of the American Civil War.[8] Therefore, while pragmatists may not explicitly challenge the notion that justice metaphysically exists, they do hold that people should avoid holding hard and fast to any specific conception of justice—as such strong commitments can cause war and the like.[9] Neo-pragmatists take this argument further and specifically hold that there is no such thing as *justice*. Instead, neo-pragmatists contend that stability is based on *intersubjective agreement*.[10] Put differently, while justice does not actually (or objectively) exist, everyone holds their own subjective concept of justice. Political stability follows from the fact that societies collectively share the same concept of justice—*intersubjective agreement*—regardless of the content of this concept.[11] Below, I rely on art (especially the Star Trek broadcast franchise) to show that justice does exist—embedded in the Hegelian *absolute*. Next, however, I treat how the profit-motive, unbridled, results in personal neurosis (*wealth addiction*) and social devastation.

WEALTH ADDICTION AND STAR TREK

Ferengis (introduced in *The Next Generation* series), as a species, elevate capitalist ideology to a religion (with their heaven being known as the Divine Treasury, and only those with sufficient profit can enter). As part of their capitalist religion/ideology, Ferengi have what are known as the "Rules of Acquisition"—a set of nostrums that Ferengis can putatively rely on in their profit-making endeavors: for example, "Exploitation begins at home"; "Expand or die"; "A wise man can hear profit in the wind." Therefore, Ferengi take the ontology of love, charity, piety that are the ostensive moral/ethical basis of religions like Christianity and Islam and replace these with a moral/ethical ontology of profit maximizing.[12]

Accumulating wealth with a religious fervor is reflective of what Vermont Senator Bernie Sanders labeled the "Billionaire Class" during his 2016 presidential run. Through entities like ALEC (American Legislative Exchange Council) and the Business Roundtable, economic elites[13] press, lobby strongly against taxation directed at corporations or the wealthy, corporate regulations, and against almost anything that seemingly interferes with the capital accumulation process.[14] Setting aside the issue of how influential such groups are in the American polity, the matter I want to focus on is this commitment among the Billionaire Class to accumulating more, more, more, and more money.[15] Why the desire to amass billions and billions of dollars?

How much can an individual consume in a lifetime? What is the purpose of having numerous homes, airplanes, automobiles?

Sam Polk, a former Wall Street trader, in 2014 published an op-ed piece in the *New York Times* where he argues *wealth addiction*[16] is rampant among the upper echelon of the American financial community.[17] Prior to coming to Wall Street, Polk was a recovering drug addict. This experience as a drug addict, he argues, allowed him to see and diagnosis himself and others as literally addicted to wealth. Polk describes that even as he was making millions he "was a giant fireball of greed." "I wanted a billion dollars. It's staggering to think that in the course of five years, I'd gone from being thrilled at my first bonus—$40,000—to being disappointed when, my second year at the hedge fund, I was paid 'only' $1.5 million." Polk explains that "in the end, it was actually my absurdly wealthy bosses who helped me see the limitations of unlimited wealth." Polk was taken aback by their hostility to any effort to limit their amassing of wealth—even if such efforts could strengthen the financial system. (Polk quotes one of his unnamed superiors as stating, "I don't have the brain capacity to think about the system as a whole. All I'm concerned with is how this affects our company.") Polk concludes that his boss "was afraid of losing money, despite all that he had" and begins to determine that such fears were rooted in addiction:

> From that moment on, I started to see Wall Street with new eyes. I noticed the vitriol that traders directed at the government for limiting bonuses after the crash [of 2008]. I heard the fury in their voices at the mention of higher taxes. These traders despised anything or anyone that threatened their bonuses. Ever see what a drug addict is like when he's used up his junk? He'll do anything—walk 20 miles in the snow, rob a grandma—to get a fix. Wall Street was like that.

Polk holds that upon leaving Wall Street he suffered "withdrawal" symptoms.

Polk argues that just like the addict is indifferent, blind to the pain and suffering he causes in feeding his addiction, much of America's economic elite is similarly unconcerned by the social, economic distress being caused by the operation of neoliberal capitalism (e.g., the unregulated movement of capital worldwide):

> Only a wealth addict would feel justified in receiving $14 million in compensation—including an $8.5 million bonus—as the McDonald's C.E.O., Don Thompson, did in 2012, while his company then published a brochure for its work force on how to survive on their low wages. Only a wealth addict would earn hundreds of millions as a hedge-fund manager, and then lobby to maintain a tax loophole that gave him a lower tax rate than his secretary.

Indifference to the social effects of a profit-making regime is conveyed in the *Star Trek: Voyager* (1995–2001) episode "False Profits" (1996). A pair of Ferengi (Arridor and Kol) manipulate a planet's religious beliefs to install themselves as its leaders. Before the arrival of the Ferengis the native population (we are told) was "flourishing." Under the Ferengis' profit-making regime the Feregni become very wealthy, and at the same time poverty proliferates among the native population. ("The two Ferengi live in a palatial temple, while the people are lucky to have a roof over their heads.") Arridor and Kol are completely inured to the suffering they've caused, only celebrating the wealth they've accumulated.

Another case of wealth addiction is portrayed in the *Star Trek: The Next Generation* (1987–1994) episode "The Neutral Zone" (1988). A capitalist, Ralph Offenhouse, from the late twentieth century is awoken from a cryogenic sleep. Immediately, Offenhouse's mind turns to his money: "I have a substantial portfolio. It's critical I check on it." Later, he adds "I have to phone Geneva right away about my accounts. The interest alone could be enough to buy even this ship." Subsequently, Captain Picard informs Ralph that "a lot has changed in three hundred years. People are no longer obsessed with the accumulation of 'things.' We have eliminated hunger, want, the need for possessions. We have grown out of our infancy." Ralph: "You've got it wrong. It's never been about 'possessions'—it's about power." Significantly, Polk in his op-ed piece holds that "Wall Street is a toxic culture that encourages the grandiosity of people who are desperately trying to feel powerful." Picard asks Ralph, "Power to do what?"

Ralph: To control your life, your destiny.

Picard: That kind of control is an illusion.

This notion of *controlling your life, your destiny* is particularly illusory in a context where the planet is warming dangerously and the biosphere is becoming destabilized as a result. Saliently, the wealth accumulation process is at the core of this planetary warming and destabilization.[18] Again, like drug addicts, wealth addicts are inured to the immense damage that their addiction causes others and themselves. The *Voyager* episode "Future's End" (1996) features a technology capitalist (Ed Starling) who in 1996 threatens to destroy Los Angeles and is mute to the fact that his effort to travel into the future to bolster the fortunes of his corporation will destroy the solar system in the twenty-ninth century.

The *Star Trek: Deep Space Nine* (1993–1999) episode "Past Tense" (1995) depicts the social misery caused by global neoliberalism. The characters Sisko, Bashir, and Dax are accidentally sent back to 2024 San Francisco. Upon being beamed to the past, Sisko and Bashir are separated from Dax.

Without any identification (or money) Sisko and Bashir are forcibly interned in an urban detainment camp for the poor and dispossessed. It is described in the script notes as follows:

> Sisko and Bashir ENTER a street lined by dirty, dilapidated buildings, with boarded up windows and impromptu campsites set up in the doorways and stairwells. It's a sharp contrast to the relatively clean city outside. The street is crowded with poorly dressed homeless men, women, and children, of all ages and races, many standing in a long food line.[19]

Sisko, who is knowledgeable about twenty-first century Earth, explains that "by the early twenty-twenties there was a place like this in every major city in the United States."

Bashir: Why are these people in here? Are they criminals?

Sisko: No. People with criminal records weren't allowed in the Sanctuary Districts.

Bashir: Then what did they do to deserve this?

Sisko: Nothing. They're just people. People without jobs or places to live.

Bashir: So they get put in here?

Sisko: Welcome to the twenty-first century.

Writing in the mid-1990s about internment camps for the poor and homeless being in place in every major American city within thirty years is an explicit critique of the neoliberal project, which was well established by the 1990s.[20] Neoliberalism has been devastating to numerous U.S. urban centers, particularly in the former industrial American heartland.[21] Cities like Detroit[22] and Cleveland[23]—which were global centers of industrial production—have been hollowed out as the U.S. manufacturing base has been shifted to cheap wage venues in the U.S. South, Mexico, China, and so on.[24] One of the displaced residents of the San Francisco Sanctuary District explains that "I used to be a Plant Manager at ChemTech Industries." The result has been pronounced urban decay in once wealthy and prosperous cities,[25] where a substantial homeless population is an enduring phenomenon.[26]

Moreover, the Great Recession of 2008 has caused persistently high unemployment.[27] A historically destabilizing factor of capitalism is the tendency of capital equipment (i.e., technology) to replace labor.[28] In a 2012 op-ed piece in the *New York Times*, Princeton economist Paul Krugman holds "there's no question that in some high-profile industries, technology is displacing workers of all, or almost all, kinds."[29] A Sanctuary District resident explains that "I came to San Francisco to work in a brewery . . . but they laid a bunch of us off when they got some new equipment . . . and so I ended up here." Another of the characters in "Past Tense" notes that "right now jobs are hard to come by . . . what with the economy and all." The former plant manager plaintively explains: "Most of us agreed to live here [in the San Francisco Sanctuary District] because they promised us jobs. I don't know about you, but I haven't been on any job interviews lately. And neither has anyone else. They've forgotten about us."

Therefore, Star Trek indicates that unbridled greed is pernicious, and can result in wealth addiction—as indicated with the Feregni (who elevate profit making to a religion) and Ralph Offenhouse (who obsesses about his financial holdings). Moreover, a society predicated on neoliberalism and the unrelenting pursuit of wealth, profit results in widespread social misery, as conveyed in the episodes "False Profits" and "Past Tense." According to Star Trek, humanity overcomes neoliberalism through the progressive dialectic—first theorized by Karl Marx and later acted upon by the Russian revolutionary Leon Trotsky.

Star Trek and Progressive Dialectic

As already noted, Star Trek explicitly rejects capitalism in "The Neutral Zone." Ralph realizes that "[t]here's no trace of my money—my office is gone—what will I do? How will I live?" Picard explains, "Those material needs no longer exist." Ralph, invoking the values of the late twentieth century, responds by asking, "Then what's the challenge?" Picard, seemingly outlining the values of twenty-fourth-century Earth, retorts: "To improve yourself . . . enrich yourself. Enjoy it, Mister Offenhouse."

Similarly, in the *Deep Space Nine* episode "In the Cards" (1997), Jake Sisko exclaims, "I'm Human, I don't have any money." Nog, a Ferengi, is critical of twenty-fourth-century humanity: "It's not my fault that your species decided to abandon currency-based economics in favor of some philosophy of self-enhancement." Shifting humanity's (America's) values away from "currency-based economics" and toward a "philosophy of self-enhancement" mirrors Karl Marx's point that in moving from capitalism to communism, society would go "[f]rom each according to his ability, to each according to his needs!"—that is, communist politics would focus on "the all-around development of the individual."[30] Or as Jake told Nog, "There's nothing wrong with our philosophy. We work to better ourselves and the rest of Humanity."

Indicative of how humans in the twenty-fourth century have undergone a profound paradigm shift in values and outlook, Quark (also a Ferengi) travels back to mid-twentieth-century Earth (more specifically, the United States), and concludes from his dealings with humans (Americans) in this epoch, that "these humans, they're not like the ones from the [twenty-fourth century] Federation. They're crude, gullible and greedy."[31] Marx offers a consonant rebuke of the cultural/social ethos of capitalists: "Contempt for theory, art, history, and for man as an end in himself . . . is the real, conscious standpoint, the virtue of the man of money."[32]

Therefore, Star Trek takes the Enlightenment to its logical conclusion—namely, that modernity, science, and reason can serve as the basis for a peaceful, highly productive, and thriving world.[33] Star Trek is optimistic insofar as arguing that as global society accepts modernity, reason, and science (i.e., the progressive dialectic), humans will collectively achieve a higher plane of intelligence, knowledge, and emotional maturity. (An optimism shared by Marx: in "communist society . . . the all-round development of the individual" will be achieved.[34]) This higher plane of existence, however, requires the overthrow of the neoliberal order.

Neoliberalism

To the American Revolutionary War (see below), the U.S. Civil War (see below), and the American fight against Fascism,[35] Star Trek adds to America's revolutionary "moments" with the *Bell Uprising*. Aired in 1995, "Past Tense" is centered on this fictional uprising. As noted above, what Sisko, Bashir, and Dax encounter in 2024 is a United States marked with extreme poverty and widespread economic displacement.

The overriding need to pursue societal justice (i.e., topple neoliberalism/capitalism) is made clear in "Past Tense." While in the Sanctuary District (in 2024 San Francisco), Sisko intervenes into a fight, which accidently results in the death of one Gabriel Bell—the would-be leader of the Bell Uprising. Like the victory of the Nazis in World War II ("City on the Edge of Forever" 1967—original series), this erases the entire history of the Federation. Meanwhile, back in the twenty-fourth century, all that remains of the original time line is the ship (the Defiant) that beamed Sisko, Bashir, and Dax to the past. Uncertain when Sisko et al. are located, members of the Defiant crew randomly transport into Earth's past. They conclude Sisko et al. "arrived before the year twenty-forty-eight."

> How can you be sure?

> Because we were just there. And that wasn't the mid-twenty-first century that I read about in school. It's been changed. *Earth history had its rough patches, but never that rough.*

Therefore, the absence of the Bell Uprising to spark the revolution that would politically challenge the current neoliberalism regime would ostensibly result in Earth's society devolving into some type of nightmare scenario as early as 2048. One is reminded of Rosa Luxemburg's pronouncement that the "future is either socialism or barbarism."[36]

The original time line is restored when Sisko takes the name Gabriel Bell, and fulfills his role in history. One of the successes of the Bell Uprising was the ability of residents of the Sanctuary District to evade a government blockade of the "Interface" (i.e., the internet—which was a nascent technology when "Past Tense" aired in 1995) and convey their personal stories to the world. One resident explains, "My name is Henry Garcia . . . and I've been living here two years now. . . . I've never been in trouble with the law or anything. . . . I don't want to hurt anybody. . . . I just want a chance to work and live like regular people."

Confirming the interpretation of Star Trek as positing American history as a series of progressive events ("revolutions") are the original series (1966–1969) episodes "The Savage Curtain" (1969) and "The Omega Glory" (1968). The episode "The Omega Glory" depicts a world with an identical history to that of Earth's, except in this instance the Cold War resulted in globally devastating nuclear/biological war—where humans were reduced to a veritable stone age. Captain Kirk ultimately realizes that the segment of the population that represented the West views the U.S. Constitution as a sacred document. But they cannot read it, so Kirk explains to them: "That which you called Ee'd Plebnista was not written for chiefs or kings or warriors or the rich and powerful, but for all the people!" Kirk proceeds to read directly from this document (the Ee'd Plebnista), which is the Constitution:

> We the people of the United States, in order to form a more perfect union, establish justice, ensure domestic tranquillity, provide for the common defense, promote the general welfare, and secure the blessings of liberty to ourselves and our posterity . . . do ordain and establish this constitution.

Asserting the revolutionary implications of the American Revolution and the Constitution that followed, Kirk declares "these words and the words that follow. . . . They must apply to everyone or they mean nothing!" Kirk adds, "[L]iberty and freedom have to be more than just words."

In "The Savage Curtain," the Enterprise crew meets the incarnation of Abraham Lincoln—the leader of what many consider to be the second American Revolution (i.e., the victorious Northern Cause in the U.S. Civil War).[37] This episode is thoroughly treated in chapter 3.

Thus, Star Trek is optimistic in that America is evolving toward an ideal, classless society. The American Revolution, the Civil War, and the Bell Uprising (i.e., the defeat of neoliberalism) are necessary stops on this road to (worldwide) utopia. This is reflective of American Marxists' view that United States' history is an unfolding revolutionary process, the end result of which is the establishment of an ideal socialist/communist society. Sidney Hook, for instance, writing in 1933 (when he was still a follower of Leon Trotsky—a Trotskyist) reasoned that "America had gone through her second revolution to break up the semi-feudal slavocracy which barred the expansion of industrial capitalism."[38] Operating in the United States since the 1920s, Trotskyists hold that the American Revolution and the Civil War remain incomplete until the worker state is in place.[39] Put differently, these revolutions will be completed by the socialist revolution (the Bell Uprising[?]). (It is noteworthy and significant that in the episode where the Bell Uprising is conveyed the phrase "Neo-Trotskists" is used; also, in another episode, a passage from the Communist Manifesto is read.[40])

CONCLUSION

Hegel, in philosophizing about the *absolute*, posited that societies could fall into "bad infinities"—where a society is alienated from the love, honesty, compassion, and so on, of the absolute. Such a society would be dominated by such values as greed and self-centeredness. The financial community, and the Billionaire Class, are ostensibly dominated by greed. Sam Polk, himself a former Wall Street trader and drug addict, holds that he witnessed the upper echelons of the U.S. financial community in the throes of wealth addiction. Under the sway of such addiction Wall Street is inured to the social misery created by the neoliberalism they handsomely profit off of. Star Trek artistically conveys wealth addiction and its pernicious individual, social, and political outcomes.

Marx's contribution to Hegelian philosophy is the argument that a society, economy governed by the *spirit of greed* is essentially politically unstable. Therefore, Marx refutes the pragmatism and neo-pragmatism ideas that political stability can be achieved within a capitalist framework. Marx is optimistic in that the inherent instabilities (*contradictions*) in capitalism will result in the forward movement of society—that is, the forward movement of the *progressive dialectic*. Through such episodes as the "Omega Glory," "Savage Curtain," and "Past Tense," the Star Trek franchise portrays the progressive dialectic and casts it as centered in the United States—consistent with the American Trotskyist worldview.

In the next chapter I demonstrate that Star Trek is predicated on Hegelian philosophy. Thus, I show an approach to Star Trek rooted in analytic philosophy elides the normative core of the franchise.

NOTES

1. Adam Smith, *The Wealth of Nations* (New York: Bantam, 2003 [1776]).

2. (*Deep Space Nine*—"Prophet Motive" 1995).
3. Eric Rauchway, *The Great Depression and the New Deal: A Very Short Introduction* (New York: Oxford University Press, 2008).
4. Jeffrey L. Chidester and Paul Kengor, eds., *Reagan's Legacy in a World Transformed* (Cambridge, MA: Harvard University Press, 2015); Doug Rossinow, *The Reagan Era: A History of the 1980s* (New York: Columbia University Press, 2015).
5. Gérard Duménil and Dominique Lévy, *Capital Resurgent: Roots of the Neoliberal Revolution*, trans. Derek Jeffers (Cambridge, MA: Harvard University Press, 2004); Daniel Stedman Jones, *Masters of the Universe: Hayek Friedman, and the Birth of Neoliberal Politics* (Princeton: Princeton University Press, 2012).
6. Hans-Johann Glock, *What Is Analytic Philosophy?* (New York: Cambridge University Press, 2008; Stephen P. Schwartz, *A Brief History of Analytic Philosophy: From Russell to Rawls* (Hoboken, NJ: Wiley-Blackwell, 2012).
7. Carlin Romano, *America the Philosophical* (New York: Simon & Schuster, 2012).
8. Louis Menand, *The Metaphysical Club* (New York: Farrar, Straus, and Giroux, 2001), xii.
9. Arguably, the most trenchant critique of pragmatism is made in the original series episode "Bread and Circuses" (1968), where the argument is made that an overriding emphasis on societal stability would result in the persistence of slavery worldwide. The Enterprise crew comes upon a planet that is virtually identical to mid-twentieth-century Earth (America); except, on this world, the Roman Empire never collapsed and, instead, spans the entire planet. "A world ruled by emperors who can trace their line back 2,000 years to their own Julius and Augustus Caesars." The result is that slavery continues—in part because the slave system was reformed (guaranteed pensions, health care) to maintain its stability. In defending this society, one of the characters explains: "This is an ordered world, a conservative world based on time-honored Roman strengths and virtues. . . . There's been no war here for over 400 years." "Could your land of that same era make that same boast?," he asks of the Enterprise landing party (specifically Kirk and McCoy).
10. Richard Rorty, *Philosophy and the Mirror of Nature* (Princeton: Princeton University Press, 1981); Michael Bacon, *Richard Rorty: Pragmatism and Political Liberalism* (Lanham, MD: Lexington Books, 2007); Neil Gross, *Richard Rorty: The Making of an American Philosopher* (Chicago: University of Chicago Press, 2008).
11. American philosopher Richard Rorty writing in the early 1980s, in fashioning *neopragmatism*, argues that societies are based on *intersubjective agreement*. Thus, what is required for societal stability is enough consensus or a set of ideas—any set of ideas. Hence, what matters is consensus, and not the ideas themselves. Presumably, when there is not enough intersubjective consensus/agreement, then social/political breakdown occurs. Rorty, *Philosophy and the Mirror of Nature*.
Over ten years before Rorty published his path-breaking notion of *intersubjective agreement*, the *Star Trek* original series episode "Mirror, Mirror," (1967) aired. Members of the Enterprise crew (including Kirk and McCoy), through a technical glitch, are beamed to an alternate universe. The Enterprise (including Spock) exists in this alternate universe, but instead of the Federation, the political authority is the "Empire"—where "behavior and discipline" is "brutal, savage." The Captain Jonathan Archer (*Star Trek: Enterprise*) from the alternative universe declares that "[g]reat men are not peacemakers. Great men are conquerors" ("In a Mirror, Darkly," 2005). The implication of "Mirror, Mirror" and ' In a Mirror, Darkly" is irrespective of their value system—whether "Empire" or "Federation"—humans can create and lead a vast interstellar political formation. Technological progress and political stability would essentially be the same.
12. Adam Kotsko, *Neoliberalism's Demons: On the Political Theology of Late Capital* (Stanford: Stanford University Press, 2018).
13. Clyde W. Barrow, *Critical Theories of the State* (Madison: University of Wisconsin Press, 1993), 17; Barrow explains that "corporations emerged as the dominant economic institutions in capitalist societies by the end of the nineteenth century." He goes on to note that as early as the late 1920s "the bulk of U.S. economic activity, whether measured in terms of assets, profits, employment, investment, market shares, or research and development, was

concentrated in the fifty largest financial institutions and five hundred largest nonfinancial corporations" (ibid.). Also see Patricia Cohen, "Study Finds Global Wealth Is Flowing to the Richest," *New York Times*, January 19, 2015, B6; Thomas Piketty, *Capital in the Twenty-First Century*, trans. Arthur Goldhammer (Cambridge, MA: Belknap Press, 2014); Clyde W. Barrow, *Toward a Critical Theory of States: The Poulantzas-Miliband Debate after Globalization* (Albany: State University of New York Press, 2016).

Political scientists Jeffrey A. Winters and Benjamin I. Page, writing in 2009, hold that "it is now appropriate to . . . think about the possibility of *extreme* political inequality, involving great political influence by a very small number of extremely wealthy individuals." They go on to add that "we argue that it is useful to think about the U.S. political system in terms of oligarchy." Jeffrey A. Winters and Benjamin I. Page, "Oligarchy in the United States," *Perspectives on Politics*, vol. 7, no. 4 (2009): 744, emphasis in original; also see Paul Krugman, "Oligarchy, American Style," *New York Times*, November 4, 2011, A31; and "The Undeserving Rich," *New York Times*, January 20, 2014, A17; Jeffrey A. Winters, *Oligarchy* (New York: Cambridge University Press, 2011); Shaila Dewan and Robert Gebeloff, "One Percent, Many Variations," *New York Times*, January 15, 2012, A1; David Leonhardt, "All for the 1%, 1% for All," *New York Times*, May 4, 2014, MM23; Nicholas Kristof, "An Idiot's Guide to Inequality," *New York Times*, July 24, 2014, A27; Anna Bernasek, "The Typical Household, Now Worth a Third Less," *New York Times*, July 27, 2014, BU6; Neil Irwin, "Economic Expansion for Everyone? Not Anymore," *New York Times*, September 27, 2014, B1; Robert Frank, "Another Widening Gap: The Haves vs. the Have-Mores," *New York Times*, November 16, 2014, BU4.

14. G. William Domhoff, *Who Rules America?* 7th ed. (New York: McGraw-Hill, 2014), chap. 4; Mike McIntire, "Nonprofit Acts as a Stealth Business Lobbyist," *New York Times*, April 22, 2012, A1.

15. Christopher Ingraham, "The Richest 1 Percent Now Owns More of the Country's Wealth than at Any Time in the Past 50 Years," *Washington Post*, December 6, 2017. Web.

16. Philip E. Slater, *Wealth Addiction* (New York: Dutton, 1980).

17. Sam Polk, "For the Love of Money," *New York Times*, January 19, 2014, SR1.

18. George A. Gonzalez, *Urban Sprawl, Global Warming, and the Empire of Capital* (Albany: State University of New York Press, 2009); Adrian Parr, *The Wrath of Capital: Neoliberalism and Climate Change Politics* (New York: Columbia University Press, 2013); Hiroko Tabuchi, "The Banks Putting Rain Forests in Peril," *New York Times*, December 4, 2016, BU1.

19. http://www.st-minutiae.com/academy/literature329/457.txt.

20. Duménil and Lévy, *Capital Resurgent*; Jones, *Masters of the Universe*.

21. Guin A. McKee, *The Problem of Jobs: Liberalism, Race, and Deindustrialization in Philadelphia* (Chicago: University of Chicago Press, 2009); Timothy Williams, "For Shrinking Cities, Destruction Is a Path to Renewal," *New York Times*, November 12, 2013, A15.

22. Thomas J. Sugrue, *The Origins of the Urban Crisis: Race and Inequality in Postwar Detroit* (Princeton: Princeton University Press, 2005); Joe Drape, "Bankruptcy for Ailing Detroit, but Prosperity for Its Terms," *New York Times*, October 14, 2013, A1.

23. Carol Poh Miller and Robert Wheeler, *Cleveland: A Concise History* (Bloomington: Indiana University Press, 2009).

24. Mary Elizabeth Gallagher, *Contagious Capitalism: Globalization and the Politics of Labor in China* (Princeton: Princeton University Press, 2005); Kelly Sims Gallagher, *China Shifts Gears: Automakers, Oil, Pollution, and Development* (Cambridge, MA: MIT Press, 2006); Louis Uchitelle, "Goodbye, Production (and Maybe Innovation)," *New York Times*, December 24, 2006, sec. 3, p. 4; Peter S. Goodman, "U.S. and Global Economies Slipping in Unison," *New York Times*, August 24, 2008, A1; David Koistinen, *Confronting Decline: The Political Economy of Deindustrialization in Twentieth-Century New England* (Gainesville: University of Florida Press, 2013).

25. Susan M. Wachter and Kimberly A. Zeuli, eds., *Revitalizing American Cities* (Philadelphia: University of Pennsylvania Press, 2013); Monica Davey, "A Picture of Detroit Ruin, Street by Forlorn Street," *New York Times*, February 18, 2014, A1; Jon Hurdle, "Philadelphia Forges to Plan to Rebuild from Decay," *New York Times*, January 1, 2014, B1.

26. Deborah K. Padgett, Benjamin F. Henwood, and Sam J. Tsemberis, *Housing First: Ending Homelessness, Transforming Systems, and Changing Lives* (New York: Oxford University Press, 2015); Craig Willse, *The Value of Homelessness: Managing Surplus Life in the United States* (Minneapolis: University of Minnesota Press, 2015).

27. Kristin S. Seefedt and John D. Graham, *America's Poor and the Great Recession* (Bloomington: Indiana University Press, 2013); "Ten States Still Have Fewer Jobs since Recession," *Reuters*, March 25, 2016. Web; David Leonhardt, "We're Measuring the Economy all Wrong," *New York Times*, September 14, 2018. Web.

28. Claire Cain Miller, "Smarter Robots Move Deeper into Workplace," *New York Times*, December 16, 2014, A1; Farhad Manjoo, "Uber's Business Model Could Change Your Work," *New York Times*, January 29, 2015, B1; Zeynep Tufekci, "The Machines Are Coming," *New York Times*, April 19, 2015, SR4; Claire Cain Miller, "What's Really Killing Jobs? It's Automation, Not China," *New York Times*, December 22, 2016, A3; Alex Williams, "Robot-proofing Your Child's Future,'" *New York Times*, December 14, 2017, D1; Peter S. Goodman, "Sweden Adds Human Touch to a Robotic Future," *New York Times* December 28, 2017, A1; Liz Alderman, "Humans Wanted, But Robots Work," *New York Times*, April 17, 2018, B1; Niraj Chokshi, "Robot Cures Human Headache: Putting Together IKEA Furniture," *New York Times*, April 19, 2018, B8.

29. Paul Krugman, "Robots and Robber Barons," *New York Times*, December 10, 2012, A27.

30. Karl Marx, *The Critique of the Gotha Programme* (London: Electric Book Co., 2001 [1875]), 20.

31. (*Deep Space Nine*—"Little Green Men" 1995).

32. Karl Marx, *On the Jewish Question*, 1844, http://www.marxists.org/archive/marx/works/1844/jewish-question/.

33. Tom Rockmore, *Marx's Dream: From Capitalism to Communism* (Chicago: University of Chicago Press, 2018).

34. Marx, *The Critique of the Gotha Programme*, 20.

35. ("City on the Edge of Forever" 1967—*Star Trek*, original series).

36. Paul Frölich, *Rosa Luxemburg: Her Life and Work* (New York: Howard Fertig, 1969); Stephen Eric Bronner, *Rosa Luxemburg: A Revolutionary for Our Times* (University Park: Pennsylvania State University Press, 1993).

37. James M. McPherson, *Abraham Lincoln and the Second American Revolution* (New York: Oxford University Press, 1992); James Oakes, *Freedom National: The Destruction of Slavery in the United States* (New York: W.W. Norton & Company, 2012).

38. Sidney Hook, *Towards the Understanding of Karl Marx* (New York: John Day, 1933), 294–95.

39. James P. Cannon, *The History of American Trotskyism: Report of a Participant* (New York: Pioneer Publishers, 1944); Constance Ashton Myers, *The Prophet's Army: Trotskyists in America, 1928–1941* (Westport, CT: Greenwood Press, 1977); A. Belden Fields, *Trotskyism and Maoism: Theory and Practice in France and the United States* (New York: Praeger, 1988), chap. 4; Bryan D. Palmer, *James P. Cannon and the Origins of the American Revolutionary Left, 1890–1928* (Urbana: University of Illinois Press, 2010); Donna T. Haverty-Stacke, *Trotskyists on Trial: Free Speech and Political Persecution since the Age of FDR* (New York: New York University Press, 2016).

40. In the midst of a labor strike (*Deep Space Nine*—"Bar Association" 1996), a character reads directly from the *Communist Manifesto*: "Workers of the world, unite. You have nothing to lose but your chains."

Chapter Two

Analytic Philosophy and Star Trek

Philosopher Richard Hanley wrote *The Metaphysics of Star Trek*. Hanley describes himself as an analytic (or Anglo-American) philosopher. Hanley adds that he considers himself a proponent of *"naturalism*—roughly, the view that philosophy is and ought to be continuous with the natural sciences, since both enterprises employ the combination of reason and empirical investigation."[1] Why would a philosopher who considers his research an adjunct to the natural sciences undertake an analysis of a fictional television series? Hanley indicates he has undertaken his book as "a useful introduction to the contemporary debates concerning humankind's place in the world."[2] Again, why is Star Trek a useful venue for this purpose? Hanley never explains.

Whether Hanley intends it or not, his book can be grouped with a virtual genre within *Star Trek Studies* that adopts a hostile and captious attitude toward the franchise.[3] In chapters 3 and 4 I take up the claims against the franchise of its being pro-American, racist, and pro-imperialist. While Star Trek does replicate the clash of civilization idea,[4] the franchise is, nevertheless, progressive, internationalist, fair-minded, and anti-imperialist.

While Hanley avoids incendiary and slanderous aspersions, he does don a gratuitously critical attitude toward Star Trek. He makes picayune or nitpick quips about the Star Trek text. For instance, Hanley takes issue with the fact that Data, an android, is cast as capable of ingesting/processing food, being inebriated through the consumption of alcohol, and engaging in sex.[5] Hanley's tack in analyzing Star Trek acts as something of a killjoy—with Hanley acknowledging at one point that his treatment is boring.[6] Thus, Hanley's goal in his book is not to engage readers in the Star Trek text, but quite the opposite—to pierce the imaginative bubble that surrounds a popular franchise character (Data), and, generally, to throw cold water on plot devices used in the franchise (e.g., time travel). How does such an attitude toward a work of fiction forward the natural sciences? Does Hanley actually fear that scientists will mistake Data for a person or make an error in viewing him as a non-person? Will people wrongly believe that time travel is possible from watching Star Trek?

This is not to suggest that Star Trek's artistic choices in relation to science are beyond critique. I, myself, point out that the franchise's use of what it calls "dilithium crystals" serves to elide difficult questions—scarcity, pollution, global warming—with regard to energy. Thus, in this instance, Star Trek is inappropriately optimistic and draws on fantasy to avoid profound issues facing modernity and humanity, more broadly.[7]

I do not see how Hanley's analytic philosophy aids the natural sciences. His attitude amounts to little more than arguing that this or that is beyond our scientific means.[8] If people actually looked to analytic philosophy for guidance, they'd be demoralized and dissuaded from trying to improve upon our manipulation of the laws of physics. Thus, to argue that Data (in reality) couldn't do this or that, or holding that time travel is outside the realm of possibility, is to stifle the kind of dreaming and imagining necessary for the advancement of science.

With regard to my critique of Star Trek's dilithum crystals, they are not cast as an invention of the human mind, but a product of nature—something that has no basis in our understanding of the natural world. Thus, while humans may some day invent the equivalent of dilithium crystals, there is no reason to think that nature anywhere has "created" them—as held in Star Trek.

While Hanley's book can be looked upon as playful scholasticism, I hold it has definite political implications. In *The Politics of Star Trek*, I make the following observation:

> The Star Trek franchise taps into the prime philosophical dilemma in modern society: striving for justice (liberal humanism) or settling for stability (*pragmatism* and *neo-pragmatism*). Thus, judging from Star Trek, the modern mind (the American Mind[?]) sees that modernity can be used to establish a global regime of justice. The fear, however, is that such visions are utopian (i.e., unattainable) and/or implementing such a vision is risky insofar as an effort to revolutionize (profoundly reform) society could result in anarchy (i.e., societal/political breakdown). Reflective of these fears, within modes of thought rooted in *pragmatism* and *neopragmatism* is the idea that the best humanity can hope for is stability (i.e., sufficient *intersubjective agreement*) and should eschew universal concepts of justice.[9]

Thus, in sowing unnecessary doubts in the Star Trek text, Hanley is heightening anxieties about the feasibility of the type of social change depicted in this text.

This charge could be made of analytic philosophy *writ large*. The height of dominance of analytic philosophy in American academia coincides with the post–World War II period,[10] when New Deal state-managerialism[11] and Soviet "socialism" were in political ascendency—and people were hoping for/expecting further government involvement in regulating/replacing the free market.[12] Moreover, during the 1960s, as the Civil Rights Movement, *Star Trek*, and the student movements were communicating the public's aspirations for major, progressive social/political change, American philosophers were mostly bound up with an intellectual project of professional naysaying.[13]

Science and Star Trek

In considering whether or not analytic philosophy is actually useful to the physical sciences, I would submit that narratives like Star Trek are more valuable to the sciences than the captious tack of the analytic philosopher. Star Trek is not solely a work of technological optimism—that is, the idea that technological advancement will alone drive social/political progress.[14] In fact, Star Trek renders cautions against unchecked/unregulated scientific/technological advancement.[15] One theme that appears in the Star Trek franchise is eugenics. In Star Trek histiography in the Earth's past (or our near future) there is a Eugenics War—"an improved breed of human. That's what the Eugenics War was all about." The war resulted when "young supermen" seized "power simultaneously in over forty nations. . . . They were aggressive, arrogant. They began to battle among themselves."[16] As a result of this experience, human genetic engineering is banned in the fictional world of Star Trek. The other prime caution that Star Trek yields against "technologism" (i.e., an uncritical faith in science/engineering) is the Borg. The Borg (first appearing in *The Next Generation*) embraces technology to such an extreme extent that they replace large parts of their body (and brain) with gadgets. (Every Borg is mechanically altered—by force if necessary.) The result is the Borg do not create knowledge, but can only appropriate (i.e., "assimilate") it from others.[17] Hence, a prominent argument in Star Trek is that if technological development is to serve as a basis for justice, freedom, and societal well-being, humanity must get its politics "right"—otherwise technological/scientific advancement can result in eugenics, for instance, or other inherently oppressive/destructive outcomes (e.g., the Borg). Therefore, Star Trek helps us to cogitate about which technologies/advancements to pursue (or not) and how to apply them (or not).[18]

Conversely, Hanley's treatment of Star Trek offers little to no guidance for the sciences, including the psychological sciences. For instance, referencing an episode where Kirk is spilt into two people—one representing his reasoning faculties and the other his emotions—Hanley delves into a discussion on the human "mind." He explains that human personality and desires are driven by a combination of emotion and reason. Hanley holds that pondering the ideal mix of emotion and reason in decision making will not guide us toward any particular goal. Thus, according to Hanley, his musings can apply to a selfless healer or a serial killer.[19] As explained in the next section, Star Trek does suggest why a good emotion/reason balance is important: to know the *absolute*.

Emotion and Reason in Star Trek

Star Trek indicates that those with a good reason/emotion equilibrium can most readily perceive the *absolute*, and act on its knowledge and be motivated by its justice.[20] Thus, both captains Kirk and Picard (for instance) are paragons of the proper admixture of emotion and reason. Broadly speaking, Star Trek is optimistic insofar as arguing that as global society accepts modernity, reason, and science (i.e., the Enlightenment) humans will collectively achieve a higher plane of intelligence, knowledge, and emotional maturity. While Data declares on numerous occasions that he lacks emotion, he does act on the desire (an emotion) to complete missions, to carry out orders, protect the innocent, and so on. It would appear that the success of the character Data (artistically speaking) is in significant part derived from his being written with the appropriate balance between reason and emotion.

Moreover, in "Transfigurations" (1990—*Next Generation*), Star Trek makes the explicit argument that those with the appropriate zen can see and possibly even become the absolute. "John Doe," as he regains his memories and bearings, is finally able to transform into seemingly the *whole*—the absolute. (John: "My species is on the verge of a wondrous evolutionary change. A transmutation beyond our physical being. I am the first of my kind to approach this metamorphosis." "My people are about to embark upon a new realm, a new plane of existence.") The character is cast as possessing a quality of peace and kindness. (Dr. Crusher to John: "I don't believe you're capable of harming any[one]."

In contrast to John Doe, who seemingly achieves the ideal balance between emotion and reason (or zen) and ostensibly comes to completely know (perhaps become) the absolute, Commander Sunad of Zalkon—who demands John be killed—is dominated by "fear" of social change. ("The Zalkonians are afraid of John.") They are fearful that John's transformation is subversive. Sunad charges that John "is a disruptive influence. He spreads lies. He encourages dissent. He disturbs the natural order of our society." (John: Zalkon's "leaders . . . claimed we were dangerous so they destroyed anyone who exhibited the signs of the transfiguration.")

Sunad's fear prevents him from embracing the fact that John has achieved a higher plane of existence, and when John offers him the knowledge of this existence ("Let me show you"), Sunad rejects it ("Don't touch me!"). Sunad "feels personally threatened by John." Thus, Sunad's instrumental reason[21] (i.e., his desire for political authority, high social status, and social/political stability as an end unto itself) prevents him from literally seeing/knowing the absolute.

While "Transfigurations" suggests the existence of the absolute, the *Voyager* episode "Sacred Ground" (1996) makes direct reference to the existence of "spirits"—a term Hegel himself would use to denote something beyond material existence. During the episode, the following is said to Janeway: "Mathematics. I can see why you enjoyed it. Solve a problem, get an answer. The answer's either right or wrong. It's very *absolute*." A veiled reference to Hegel's philosophy? Indicative of Hegelian reasoning the following point is made: "Real is such a relative term." Janeway's materialist (i.e., analytic philosophy) thinking is described in the following: "That would be nice and quantifiable for you, wouldn't it. If the spirits were something you could see and touch and scan with your little devices." Overtly critiquing Kantian rationalism,[22] the following is said to Janeway: "There you go again, always looking for a rational explanation. Well there isn't one."

The action of "Sacred Ground" centers on the fact that Kes (a Voyager crew member) becomes incapacitated when she comes into contact with an "energy field." Voyager's doctor is unable to bring Kes out of her coma and she's on the verge of death. Unable to find a scientific explanation for the field or Kes's condition, Captain Janeway is forced to appeal to the "monks" that oversee the energy field. They consider it a manifestation of their deities—the *Ancestral Spirits*. In order to save Kes, Janeway is told "that the only thing that matters is finding your connection to the spirits."[23] In the end, it is only when Janeway accepts that something beyond material reality exists (i.e., the *Ancestral Spirits*) that Kes is revived.

Star Trek indicates that the zen required to know the absolute is achieved through honesty, selflessness, and a commitment to intellectual, scientific discovery/knowledge. These are the values at the core of the Federation. Captain Picard declares that "[t]he first duty of every Starfleet officer is to the *truth*. Whether it's scientific truth, or historical truth, or personal truth. *It is the guiding principle upon which Starfleet is based.*"[24] (Starfleet is the military institution of the Federation.) Indicating the selfless politics and economics of twenty-third century humanity, Kirk explains to someone in the early twentieth century that "*Let me help*" in "[a] hundred years or so from now, I believe, a famous novelist will write a classic using that theme. He'll recommend those three words even over '*I love you*.'"[25] In making the case for a federated interstellar political system to an audience of delegates of the would-be United Federation of Planets, Captain Archer (*Star Trek: Enterprise* [2001–2005]) emphasizes the overriding importance of space exploration and expanding scientific knowledge:

> Up until about a hundred years ago, there was one question that burned in every human, that made us study the stars and dream of traveling to them, Are we alone? Our generation is privileged to know the answer to that question. We are all explorers, driven to know what's over the horizon, what's beyond our own shores. And yet, the more I've experienced, the more I've learned that no matter how far we travel, or how fast we get there, the most profound discoveries are not necessarily beyond that next star. They're within us, woven into the threads that bind us, all of us, to each other. The final frontier begins in this hall. Let's explore it together.[26]

According to Star Trek, (as described in chapter 1) a society founded upon honesty, social justice, and intellectual, scientific discovery/knowledge comes about through the rejection of capitalism and the replacement of the neoliberalist world order. Thus, only through the rejection of instrumental reason as a philosophical/political foundation can a society achieve the absolute.

CONCLUSION

Star Trek is a work of science fiction. Hanley's analytic philosophy takes the science part too seriously, thereby adopting an inappropriately critical tack toward Star Trek text. It is the fiction side of the franchise that matters. Through artistic choices Star Trek's creators intelligently explore the political and social issues that confront humanity in the modern era. Despite Hanley's careful attention to the Star Trek text, this is lost to him.

In confronting these issues the makers of the franchise draw on Marxism, and posit key critiques of *pragmatism/neo-pragmatism*. Perhaps by happenstance (more likely not), Star Trek also points to Georg Hegel's reasoning and normative approach. Hegel's *absolute* is embedded in the Star Trek text. This is clearly evident in the episode "Transfiguration"—with a character achieving knowledge of the *whole*. "Sacred Ground" explicitly points to "spirits"—in the Hegelian sense—and the idea that *the real* extends beyond the material, so-called rational, realm. More than just postulating the existence of the absolute, Star Trek ostensibly makes the argument that through honesty, social justice, and a commitment to scientific, intellectual discovery people can know the absolute and bring forth its promise.

Chapters 3 and 4 address identity politics. The international prestige and standing of Abraham Lincoln indicates that people across the world want social, political harmony among all ethnic groups (chapter 3). The Star Trek franchise, itself, is proof positive of the public's desire for global unity (chapter 4).

NOTES

1. Richard Hanley, *The Metaphysics of Star Trek* (New York: Basic Books, 1997), xvi, emphasis in original.
2. Ibid., xvii.
3. For example, Rick Worland, "Captain Kirk: Cold Warrior," *Journal of Popular Film & Television* 16, no. 3 (1988): 109–117; Mark P. Lagon, "'We Owe It to Them to Interfere': *Star Trek* and U.S. Statecraft in the 1960s and the 1990s," in *Political Science Fiction*, Donald M. Hassler and Clyde Wilcox, eds. (Columbia: University of South Carolina Press, 1997); Daniel Leonard Bernardi, *Star Trek and History: Race-ing toward a White Future* (New Brunswick, NJ: Rutgers University Press, 1998); Keith M. Booker, "The Politics of Star Trek," in *The Essential Science Fiction Reader*, J. P. Telotte, ed. (Lexington: University Press of Kentucky, 2008).
4. Samuel P. Huntington, *The Clash of Civilizations and the Remaking of World Order* (New York: Simon & Schuster, 1996); Martin Hall and Patrick Thaddeus Jackson, eds., *Civilization Identity* (New York: Palgrave Macmillan, 2007).
5. Hanley, *The Metahpysics of Star Trek*, 59–64.
6. Ibid., 33.
7. George A. Gonzalez, *The Politics of Star Trek: Justice, War, and the Future* (New York: Palgrave Macmillan, 2015), chap. 8.
8. Hans-Johann Glock, *What Is Analytic Philosophy?* (New York: Cambridge University Press, 2008).
9. Gonzalez, *The Politics of Star Trek*, 115.
10. Carlin Romano, *America the Philosophical* (New York: Simon & Schuster, 2012); Stephen P. Schwartz, *A Brief History of Analytic Philosophy: From Russell to Rawls* (Hoboken, NJ: Wiley-Blackwell, 2012).
11. Eric Rauchway, *The Great Depression and the New Deal: A Very Short Introduction* (New York: Oxford University Press, 2008).
12. Robert A. Dahl and Charles E. Lindblom, "Preface" in *Politics, Economics, and Welfare* (New Haven, CT: Yale University Press, 1976).
13. John McCumber, *Time in a Ditch: American Philosophy in the McCarthy Era* (Evanston, IL: Northwestern University Press, 2001), and *The Philosophy Scare: The Politics of Reason in the Early Cold War* (Chicago: University of Chicago Press, 2016).
14. Gérard Klein, "From the Images of Science to Science Fiction," in *Learning from Other Worlds*, Patrick Parrinder, ed. (Durham, NC: Duke University Press, 2001).
15. Alan Shapiro, *Star Trek: Technologies of Disappearance* (Berlin: Avinus Press, 2004).
16. (*Star Trek*, original series—"Space Seed" 1967).
17. "The Borg gain knowledge through assimilation. What they can't assimilate, they can't understand" (*Star Trek: Voyager*—"Scorpion" 1997).
18. Nicholas Wade, "Scientists Seek Ban on Method of Editing the Human Genome," *New York Times*, March 20, 2015, A1.
19. Hanley, *The Metaphysics of Star Trek*, 5–10.
20. David S. Stern, ed., *Essays on Hegel's Philosophy of Subjective Spirit* (Albany: State University of New York Press, 2013).
21. Darrow Schecter, *The Critique of Instrumental Reason from Weber to Habermas* (New York: Bloomsbury Academic, 2012); Max Horkheimer, *Critique of Instrumental Reason*, trans. Matthew O'Connell (New York: Verso, 2013).
22. In the *Critique of Pure Reason*, Kant argues that reason and empiricism can account for all phenomena. Immanuel Kant, *Critique of Pure Reason*, trans. Max Muller (New York: Penguin, 2008 [1781]).
23. Two observers hold that the religious idea conveyed in the *Voyager* episode "Sacred Ground" is consonant with New Age beliefs, "that spiritual experience are a response to individual spiritual needs and interpretations." Darcee L. McLaren and Jennifer E. Porter, "(Re)Covering Sacred Ground: New Age Spirituality in Star Trek: *Voyager*," in *Star Trek and Sacred Ground: Explorations of Star Trek, Religion, and American Culture*, Jennifer E. Porter and Darcee L. McLaren, eds. (Albany: State University of New York Press, 1999), 108.

24. (*Next Generation*—"The First Duty" 1992). When Captain Kirk in *Star Trek Beyond* (2016) is caught lying to Starfleet he is stripped of his captaincy.
25. (*Star Trek*, original series—"City on the Edge of Forever" 1967).
26. (*Enterprise*—"Terra Prime" 2005).

Chapter Three

Abraham Lincoln as Globalist

Lincoln before Lincoln by Brian J. Snee is a survey analysis of broadcast treatments of Abraham Lincoln prior to Steven Spielberg's 2012 movie *Lincoln*. Snee's most significant finding is that prior to Spielberg's movie, Lincoln as "Great Emancipator" is underplayed, if not totally ignored, in the numerous cinematic and television representations of the 16th U.S. president. Snee explains that "Beginning with D. W. Griffith's *The Birth of a Nation*—an overtly racist film that laments the demise of the Confederacy and celebrates the formation of the Ku Klux Klan—Hollywood routinely minimized or simply ignored Lincoln's role as the emancipator."[1]

Here, I hold that Snee unduly overlooks the treatment that Lincoln received in the *Star Trek* (original series) episode "Savage Curtain" (1969). Snee only writes about Lincoln's appearance in "Savage Curtain" as being "absurdly creative"[2] (whatever that means). Star Trek's Lincoln is arguably the most important popular representation of the man as the franchise is ostensibly the most popular in U.S. television history—and "Savage Curtain" has been replayed literally innumerable (or countless) times worldwide. Unlike other television and movie portrayals of Lincoln (outside of Spielberg's *Lincoln*), Star Trek's creators convey him as a figure of immense historic, global importance.

Snee's somewhat dismissive attitude toward the portrayal of Lincoln in Star Trek is consonant with a broader caustic, captious tack evident in the literature on Star Trek. The field of *Star Trek Studies* has been maligned by two hugely flawed assumptions: (1) that the original series is a metaphor for the Cold War (professor of U.S. television history, Rick Worland: "the Klingons and the Federation were firmly established as two ideologically opposed superpower blocs"[3]), and, even more egregious, (2) that the Federation represents a kind of pro-American political trope (professor of international relations, Mark P. Lagon: "the zealous desire of James T. Kirk, as the hero of the original *Star Trek*, to spread the Federation's way of life serves as a mirror to observe the American style of foreign policy"[4]. (English professor, M. Keith Booker: Captain "Kirk is a walking icon of Americanism."[5]) These misplaced assumptions have worked to devalue *Star Trek* as pro-American Cold War propaganda.

Lincoln's portrayal in "Savage Curtain" serves the overall globalist outlook evident in the *Star Trek* original series.[6] Contrary to the claims made by critics, *Star Trek* (the original series) is not nationalist (or pro-American), but pro-modernism. In *Star Trek* Lincoln is cast as a figure that forwarded progressive modernism—on a worldwide basis.

Lincoln in "Savage Curtain"

Lincoln comes to life in "Savage Curtain" because an alien race that the starship Enterprise has newly come into contact with wants to learn about good and evil—ideas that are foreign to them. The aliens create figures from the past of the Federation (an interstellar organization encompassing Earth)—Lincoln being one of them. The camps designated "good" and "evil" ultimately fight it out in an experiment to learn about these concepts. Lincoln is in the camp representing good.

While Lincoln was an American president, as the leader of the Northern victory over the Southern slavocracy, he is a figure of worldwide saliency. Arguably, Lincoln is the person most credited in the modern era with the defeat of feudalism in the West, and the concomitant triumph of progressive modernism.[7] The editors of the volume *The Global Lincoln* explain that "Lincoln's global celebrity lies in . . . his resolute defense of popular government and free labor."[8]

Of the avatars created to conduct the alien's experiment, Lincoln (by far) receives the most attention—as he is a guest abroad Enterprise (whereas the others are not). Significantly, James T. Kirk (captain of the Enterprise) in the twenty-third century strongly admires the personage of Lincoln, so much so that Kirk shows great deference and respect to what is obviously an ersatz Lincoln.[9] Kirk notes, "I cannot conceive it possible that Abraham Lincoln could have actually been reincarnated. And yet his kindness, his gentle wisdom, his humor, everything about him is so right." McCoy (the ship's doctor) chides Kirk: "Practically the entire crew has seen you treat this impostor like the real thing when he can't possibly be the real article. Lincoln died three centuries ago hundreds of light-years away." Spock (first officer) observes to Kirk: "President Lincoln has always been a very personal hero to you." Kirk retorts, "Not only to me." Spock: "Agreed." The fact that Kirk (and others) would admire Lincoln three hundred years after his death and in a context of world government (i.e., the United States no longer exists) in and of itself indicates that Lincoln is a figure of substantial historic and global importance.

Importantly, other than Lincoln on the "good" team is Surak—a Vulcan. He is cast as a modernizing figure for the Vulcans. Spock (a Vulcan) on Surak: "The greatest of all who ever lived on our planet, Captain. The father of all we became." Hence, Lincoln and Surak (who are teamed together along with Kirk and Spock) mirror each other—as both were world-changing figures for their respective planets.

Surak and the Vulcan back story can be read as a critique and rejection of nationalism. The fictional Vulcans actively seek to control and minimize their emotions. Spock in other episodes describes how Vulcans waged vicious wars against each other,[10] so much so that their planet would have been destroyed were it not for the movement led by Surak. This movement resulted in a Vulcan society that embraced stoicism, as well as empiricism, rationality ("logic"). Nationalism is at its base an emotion—love of country.[11] Vulcan history is an allegory of how humans in the 1960s were threatening their own planet because of the emotion of nationalism, patriotism. Hence, just like the Vulcans (led by Surak) came to reject nationalism (along with all emotions), so did humans in forming a world government, and, ultimately, the Federation. The ersatz Surak, when first meeting humans, responds in a globalist, universalist manner: "In my time, we knew not of Earth men. I am pleased to see that we have differences. May we together become greater than the sum of both of us."

Star Trek (the original series) rejected the Cold War, and the nationalisms it was predicated upon. Part of the rejection of nationalism and the Cold War in *Star Trek* is a critique of post–World War II American foreign policy. Indeed, *Star Trek* conveyed virulent nationalism (i.e., Nazism) as irrevocably rooted in hate and destined to destroy civilization.

Star Trek as Outside the Cold War

The first indication that *Star Trek* stands outside of the Cold War is the fact that in the series Earth is governed by a world government, and the United States/Soviet Union do not exist. More broadly, the series casts nationalism in a negative light. Thus, Earthlings are part of the Federation—a modernist nomenclature—an institution composed of peoples from throughout interstellar space. Notably, in Star Trek it is peoples that politically identify themselves by their ethnicity (nationalism)—the Klingons, Romulans—that are seemingly warlike and aggressive. In "Savage Curtain" on the "evil" team is the figure of Kahless—the founder of the Klingon Empire: "Kahless the Unforgettable, the Klingon who set the pattern for his planet's tyrannies." Presumably, one of his sins was establishing the Klingon state based on Klingon national identity (i.e., nationalism).

Daniel Bernardi, in *Star Trek and History: Race-ing Toward a White Future*, holds the Star Trek franchise (particularly the original series and *Next Generation*) exhibits racism—or more specifically an "anti-black" attitude (a type of "white" nationalism).[12] Focusing specifically on *Star Trek*, the original series, Lt. Uhura (played by African-American actor Nichelle Nichols) was reduced to a bit role—given almost exclusively throw away lines. Nevertheless, this character was involved in a scene conveying arguably the clearest stance for ethnic equality and acceptance ever on American television. In "The Savage Curtain" the ersatz Abraham Lincoln says to Uhura, "What a charming Negress." He quickly corrects himself, "Oh, forgive me, my dear. I know in my time some used that term as a description of property." Uhura responds "But why should I object to that term, sir? [. . .] We've each learned to be delighted with what we are."

An even clearer rejection of nationalism (Americanism—"whitism") is made by Kirk and Spock (a Vulcan) in "Whom Gods Destroy" (1969—original series). Kirk speaks of the founders of the Federation: "They were humanitarians and statesmen, and they had a dream. A dream that became a reality and spread throughout the stars, a dream that made Mister Spock and me brothers." Indicative of how the Federation transcends all ethnic, religious, and species divisions, Spock, when asked, "Do you consider Captain Kirk and yourself brothers?" replies, "Captain Kirk speaks somewhat figuratively and with undue emotion. However, what he says is logical and I do, in fact, agree with it."

Most importantly, *Star Trek* denies the validity of the normative core of the American position concerning the Cold War (i.e., anti-Communism[13]). Thus, Star Trek, far from replicating the American arguments against the Soviet Union, indicates that the Cold War is nothing more than a struggle between Great Powers over resources and territory.[14] This point is made explicit when the Klingons (the main geopolitical rival of the Federation) are first introduced in "Errand of Mercy" (1967—original series). When the Organians intervene to prevent a Klingon–Federation war, in objecting to this intervention neither Captain Kirk nor the Klingon at hand refer to the normative justifications/pretenses at the heart of the Cold War. Particularly significant is that Kirk does not refer to freedom, liberty, and so on—the typical Cold War rhetoric of the American side. Instead, Kirk's complaints are of the traditional Great Power sort: "We have legitimate grievances against the Klingons. They've invaded our territory, killed our citizens. They're openly aggressive. They've boasted that they'll take over half the galaxy." In 1987, during the pilot of *Next Generation*, *Star Trek*'s creators expressly cast the Cold War as "silly arguments about how to divide the resources" of the planet.[15] Taking the Cold War as simply an aggressive phase of great power politics, the following is a sharp rebuke of those that seemingly sought war with the Soviet Union: The Organian spokesman: "To wage war, Captain [Kirk]? To kill millions of innocent people? To destroy life on a planetary scale? Is that what you're defending [i.e., arguing for]?"

Significantly, when Star Trek does point to American normative values the suggestion is made that in the context of the Cold War, the United States has forgotten these values (McCarthyism [?]). In "The Omega Glory,"(1968—original series) the Enterprise crew encounters a planet identical to Earth except the Cold War resulted in a nuclear/biological weapons conflagration. The planet's population has been reduced to a veritable stone age. The group that represents the West (the "Yangs") worships the American Constitution (the document), but they do not know what it means (i.e., they are unable to read it). Ultimately, it is up to Kirk to remind them of the values that informed America.[16]

Again, far from accepting/conveying/replicating the normative notions that were deemed insuperable during the Cold War, Star Trek suggests that peace between the Great Powers is achievable. The following is reported in "Day of the Dove" (1968—original series): "For three years, the Federation and the Klingon Empire have been at peace." The action begins when the Enterprise rescues the crew from a Klingon vessel as it explodes. The Enterprise crew and the Klingons engage in hostilities—with hate, anger, and false accusations spewing from both sides. It turns out that they are being influenced and manipulated to hate and attack each other. "There's an alien entity aboard the ship. It's forcing us to fight." "It subsists on the emotions of others." The alien entity "appears to be strengthened by mental irradiations of hostility, violent intentions. It exists on the hate of others. To put it simply." In the end, the Klingons and the Enterprise crew join forces to vanquish the alien creating the hostilities. To the alien: "Maybe you've caused a lot of suffering, a lot of history, but that's all over." The final scene of the episode shows the Klingons and the Federation crew standing shoulder to shoulder laughing and jovial. The Organian (in "Errand of Mercy") informs Captain Kirk and the Klingon commander that in the future "you and the Klingons will become fast friends. You will work together."

The other great power in the *Star Trek* original series narrative is the Romulan Empire. The Romulans were introduced in "Balance of Terror" (1966—original series). A Romulan ship has invaded Federation space and destroyed outposts along the "Neutral Zone" (an ostensive reference to the "Demilitarized Zone" on the Korean peninsula). The Romulan "warbird" seeks to destroy the Enterprise using an invisibility ("cloaking") device. After sustaining heavy damage inflicted by the Enterprise, the captain of the ship engages its self-destruct sequence. Indicating that the chasm between the Federation and the Romulans can be bridged, the captain of the doomed ship says to Captain Kirk: "I regret that we meet in this way. You and I are of a kind. In a different reality, I could have called you friend."

A particular strike against the idea that the original *Star Trek* can be reduced to a metaphor of the Cold War is that there is nothing Soviet/Russian about the Klingons.[17] It is noteworthy that the Klingons (of the 1960s variant and beyond) look like peoples of central Asia, not Russians[18] —dark skin and dark hair. Moreover, the Klingons employ no Soviet symbols nor slogans. Unless we knew that *Star Trek*, the original series, was produced during the Cold War, we would have little reason to think that the Klingons are an allegory for the Soviet Union. Quite the contrary, highly suggestive of an attitude of detente in the original series, is the character Chekov, an Enterprise officer with a Russian/Soviet background and accent. Chekov's Russian/Soviet nationalist comments were benignly (and lightly) received by Captain Kirk and crew.

Star Trek as Critique of American Foreign Policy

Viewing Star Trek, not as metaphor of the Cold War, but as a commentary on great power politics of the era, the original series can be interpreted as offering a critical stance on the West's (U.S.'s) conduct in its competition with the Soviet Union. At a minimum, the claim is made that the United States is no better in its tactics in the underdeveloped world than the Soviets. In "Private Little War" (1968—original series), Kirk relates to a native on a primitive world that "there came a time when our weapons . . . grew faster than our wisdom, and we almost destroyed ourselves." So when the Klingons seemingly begin to supply particular tribes on this planet with advanced weapons, Kirk is reticent to do the same. In the context of U.S. involvement in Vietnam, where the American military command measured success by the number of enemy dead, McCoy's comment that "killing is stupid and useless" can be viewed as a powerful condemnation. Kirk refers explicitly to the Vietnam War: "Do you remember the twentieth-century brush wars on the Asian continent? Two giant powers involved. . . . Neither side could pull out." Drawing his inspiration from this historical precedent, Kirk concludes that the Federation will arm its allies on the planet with the same kind of weaponry given by the Klingons: "The only solution is what happened back then. Balance of power. The trickiest, most difficult, dirtiest game of them all, but the only one that preserves both sides."

In the episode "Arena" (1967—original series) it is acknowledged that the West engages in aggressive, militaristic colonization. A Federation colony in a remote region of space is attacked and Kirk is determined to destroy the offending ship to make an example of it:

Spock: You mean to destroy the alien ship, Captain?

. . .

Kirk: If the aliens go unpunished, they'll be back, attacking other Federation installations.

Spock: I merely suggested that a regard for sentient life.

Kirk: There's no time for that. It's a matter of policy. Out here, we're the only policemen around. And a crime has been committed.

Later, we learn that the matter is not as simple as Kirk believed. It turns out that the Federation colony was in Gorn space, and they viewed it as an invasion. Upon hearing the Gorn side of things, McCoy acknowledges that "we could be in the wrong" and "the Gorn simply might have been trying to protect themselves." In the end, Kirk decides to spare the life of the captain of the Gorn ship that destroyed the Federation colony.

"Patterns of Force" (1968—original series) and "A Piece of the Action" (1968—original series) can both be interpreted as critical of American intervention in *underdeveloped* societies. In "Patterns of Force" a renown Federation historian is sent to a relatively primitive planet (Ekos) as a "cultural observer." Nevertheless, in an effort to stabilize the planet's society the historian models its politics on Nazi Germany. When the historian (named Gill) is asked why he interfered in the primitive planet's politics/social organization, he responds (in a drugged stupor): "Planet . . . fragmented . . . divided. Took lesson from Earth history." "Why Nazi Germany?" as a model. Gill: "You studied history. You knew what the Nazis were. Most efficient state . . . Earth ever knew." Thus, just as the United States was doing during the Cold War in its relations with *underdeveloped* countries, Gill prioritized political stability and expediency over virtually all other values.

"A Piece of the Action" involves a remote planet (Sigma Iotia II) a Federation ship visited one hundred years ago. This contact distorted the planet's society because the ship left behind a book dealing with "Gangsters. Chicago. Mobs. Published in 1992." "They seized upon that one book as the blueprint for an entire society. As the Bible." As a result the society of Sigma Iotia II organized itself into a set of competing mafia organizations—where the mobs themselves are the government. This is similar to the distortion that occurred in *underdeveloped* countries when they were incorporated into the American world system. In many underdeveloped societies rentier/compradore classes came to dominate, as they offer raw materials and cheap labor to multi-national corporations. Such countries are characterized by corruption and authoritarian practices.[19] The following exchange in "A Piece of the Action" occurs between women on the street and a mafia lieutenant:

Women: When's the boss going to do something about the crummy street lights around here, eh? A girl ain't safe. And how about the laundry pickup? We ain't had a truck by in three weeks.

Mafia Henchman: Write him a letter.

Women: He sent it back with postage due. We pay our percentages. We're entitled to a little service for our money.

Henchman: Get lost, will ya? Some people got nothing to do but complain.

Prioritizing stability and expediency, the Enterprise crew sets on the following course: "Oxmyx is the worst gangster of all [on this planet]. We quarrel with Oxmyx' methods, but his goal is essentially the correct one. This society must become united or it will degenerate into total anarchy." Just as the New York mafia did with Costa Nostra in the 1930s,[20] the Enterprise establishes a federated political structure employing the planet's mafia groups: "You people, you've been running this planet like a piecework factory. From now on, it's going to be under one roof. You're going to run it like a business. That means you're going to make a profit."

"The Apple" (1967—original series) also raises questions about intervention into *underdeveloped* parts of the world. Visiting the planet Gamma Triaguli VI, the Enterprise crew find that the inhabitants are content living a primitive life. They are sustained by an artificial intelligence also inhabiting the planet: "I just ran a check on the natives, and there's a complete lack of harmful bacteria in their systems, no decalcification, no degeneration of tissue, no arteriosclerosis. In simple terms, they're not growing old, and I can't tell you how old they are—20 years or 20,000 years." The natives provide the machine (Vaal) with energy (food) to maintain it. McCoy objects to this arrangement but Spock objects to applying human values to the situation, regarding it as "a splendid example of reciprocity":

McCoy: It would take a computerized Vulcan mind, such as yours, to make that kind of a statement.

Spock: Doctor, you insist on applying human standards to nonhuman cultures. Humans are only a tiny minority in this galaxy.

McCoy: There are certain absolutes, and one of them is the right of humanoids to a free and unchained environment, the right to have conditions which permit growth.

Spock: Doctor, these people are healthy and they are happy. Whatever you choose to call it, this system works, despite your emotional reaction to it.

McCoy: It might work for you, Mr. Spock, but it doesn't work for me.

Kirk expresses a similar opinion in "This Side of Paradise" (1967—original series) when his crew opts under an alien influence for a bucolic, sedentary life: "Man stagnates if he has no ambition, no desire to be more than he is."

Star Trek as a Caution against Nazism

As already noted, *Star Trek* does not treat the Cold War as an irrevocable normative struggle for the future of the planet. Instead, the series creators seemingly advise the great powers of the mid-twentieth century to ramp down the tensions of the Cold War, lest they risk an unnecessary, devastating conflict.

While Star Trek does not cast Cold War communism/Stalinism as an eminent ideological threat, the series creators do strongly caution against fascism/Nazism—indicating that it is predicated on genocidal hate and poses a profound threat to civilization. "Patterns of Force," as noted above, portrays a Nazi regime on the planet of Ekos—which was instituted/sponsored/overseen by a Federation official. With Nazism as the political basis of Ekos, the Ekosians organize around the vilification of Zeons—a population from the neighboring planet of Zeon. ("Why do the Nazis hate Zeons?" "Because without us to hate, there'd be nothing to hold them together. So the Party has built us into a threat, a disease to be wiped out.") In addition to massacring the Zeons on Ekos ("the eliminations have started. Within an hour, the Zeon blight will forever be removed from Ekos"), the Nazi regime organizes a planned genocide ("Their Final Solution") against Zeons on their home planet: "Our entire solar system will forever be rid of the disease that was Zeon."

In "City on the Edge of Forever" (1967—original series) one of the Enterprise's crew members (Doctor McCoy) inadvertently goes back in time and prevents the U.S. entrance into World War II. The result being that the Nazis win the war, which subsequently prevents the formation of the Federation and even apparently stops humanity from ever being a space faring race. ("Your vessel, your beginning, all that you knew is gone.")

Star Trek's Modernist Bias

Critics of Star Trek point to episodes like "The Apple" and "This Side of Paradise" to argue that the original series does little more than replicate American values and justifies their imposition on other societies. It does not matter to these critics that in altering the politics of these "primitive" societies *Star Trek* (Spock) offers important (reflective) criticisms of these society-altering decisions. After Spock is freed from the alien (drug-induced) influence that led him to a sedentary, bucolic life in "This Side of Paradise," he says the following: "I have little to say about it, Captain, except that for the first time in my life I was happy." Professor Booker acknowledges that "Spock's point is potentially a highly subversive one, both in its rejection of capitalist competition and in its approval of drug-induced happiness." Nevertheless, Booker dismisses Spock's commentary for the odd reason that his character is "only half human," so his views "can hardly be taken as representative of Star Trek's view of the human condition."[21]

Thus, Booker rejects the idea that Star Trek is seeking to reflectively acknowledge and explore the biases in Western/modern reasoning. Instead, "the bulk of *Star Trek* tends to suggest . . . that the expansionist-colonialist impulse is natural."[22] In drawing this judgement Booker makes no mention of "The Paradise Syndrome" (1968—original series), where the Enterprise crew comes upon a group of Native American tribes transported to an alien planet. ("A mixture of Navajo, Mohican, and Delaware, I believe. All among the more advanced and peaceful tribes.") Significantly, no effort whatsoever is made to colonize or interfere with the transported natives. Instead, Kirk et al. succeed in ensuring that the tribes can continue their pre-modern existence.

An episode Booker does engage with is "Friday's Child" (1967—original series). The ostensive moral of this episode is that if the United States wants to gain the allegiance of underdeveloped societies it should respect their culture and politics. As it is the promise of political and cultural autonomy that results in a "primitive" planet's joining of the Federation camp and not that of the Klingon's. (Kirk: "The highest of all our laws states that your world is yours and will always remain yours.") Booker alleges that "Friday's Child" is pro-U.S. Cold War "propaganda": "much in the way the United States and the its allies vied with the Soviet Union and its allies in the 1960s to see which could make a more compelling case for itself as the legitimate foe of colonialism and friend of international liberation."[23] While a viewer watching in the late 1960s could share Booker's analysis of this episode, it is the obligation of the cultural critic to set aside his or her biases and assumptions in considering a work of art.

A similar charge of operating through bias/myopia can be made of Lagon's reading of "The Apple." After the Enterprise crew "free" the tribe of natives from Vaal, Kirk promises Federation assistance ("with our help") in transitioning to the point that they "learn" to "care for" themselves. Lagon, conflates this promise of help with U.S. rhetoric surrounding its foreign aid, which tend to serve American hegemonic designs:

The caveat "with our help" points to a set of complicated questions for U.S. policy: How long and at what cost will other societies require help to introduce democracy? Must they conform to our variety of democracy (limiting government intervention in economic affairs, based on a presidential rather than parliamentary system, and based on single member districts rather than proportional representation)? Should the United States use force to promote democracy?[24]

Taking the Star Trek text seriously (something I think that the likes of Bernardi, Lagon, and Booker do not do), "The Apple" makes a case for modernism, not "American democracy" per se. Kirk uses what can be viewed as Enlightenment rhetoric when assuring the natives that their lives will be better post-Vaal—in spite of the fact that the machine provided for all their needs: "You'll learn to build for yourselves, think for yourselves. . . . You'll like it, a lot."

If we're going to read humanity's politics and history into this dialogue, it appears closer to an argument against religious paternalism (as the natives worshiped Vaal), than a justification/lauding of American intervention in the *developing world*. Consistent with this interpretation, in the denouement direct reference is made to religious allegory:

Spock: Captain, you are aware of the biblical story of Genesis.

Kirk: Yes, of course I'm aware of it. Adam and Eve tasted the apple and as a result were driven out of paradise.

Spock: Precisely, Captain, and in a manner of speaking, we have given the people of Vaal the apple, the knowledge of good and evil if you will, as a result of which they too have been driven out of paradise.

Thus, it is preferable to struggle for survival and develop your mind and society as a result, than it is to live in comfort but in ignorance. Hence, despite Spock's claim that they drove the people of Vaal out of Eden, McCoy confidently holds "we put those people back on a normal course of social evolution."

In considering whether or not "The Apple" is a stealth justification/invocation for American intervention in the *developing world*, or a meditation on the merits/demerits of promoting modernity, it is apposite to ponder the episode "Mirror, Mirror" (1967—original series). "Mirror, Mirror" opens with a discussion between Kirk and the leader of the "Halkans" (named "Tharn"). The Halkans refuse to allow the Federation to mine the dilithium crystals on their planet because "dilithium crystals represent awesome power. Wrongful use of that power, even to the extent of the taking of one life, would violate our history of total peace." Kirk asks, "When may we resume discussion?" Tharn: "The council will meditate further, but do not be hopeful of any change." Tharn adds: "Captain, you do have the might to force the crystals from us, of course." Kirk: "But we won't."

Through a technical glitch, the Enterprise landing party is transported to an alternate universe. The Enterprise exists in this alternate universe, but instead of the Federation the political authority is the "Empire"—where "behavior and discipline" is "brutal, savage." While in the Federation universe the Enterprise only pursues peaceful means with the Halkans, in the Empire universe Kirk is "ordered to annihilate the Halkans unless they comply. *No alternative.*"

Booker and Lagon would presumably hold that "Mirror, Mirror" only obfuscates the fact that the United States engages in military interventions throughout the world, because the audience is suppose to associate the Federation with the United States and the Empire with the Soviet Union. Regardless, "Mirror, Mirror" is an explicit rejection/critique of military intervention into other societies—particularly for purposes of controlling natural resources. A censure that can be issued to the United States of the Cold War Era.

A critique of U.S. foreign policy can also be read into the Federation's Prime Directive. It is a policy of "Non-Interference," which expressly proscribes changing/influencing "the normal evolution" of non-Federation worlds.[25] While not always upheld by the Enterprise crew, the Prime Directive establishes that the Federation is prohibited from giving advanced technology to non-Federation planets, as well as influencing the politics/economics of said planets ("The Apple"; "Private Little War"; "Friday's Child"; "Bread and Circuses" [1968—original series]; "A Piece of the Action"). The Prime Directive would be directly at odds with Modernization Theory, embraced by foreign policy makers in the White House during the 1960s. Modernization theory amounted to a Cold War strategy to share advanced technology and foster particular economic policies within the pro-Western countries of the *developing world* in an effort to solidify their position within the American-led camp.[26]

An additional critique of American foreign policy can be found in "Savage Curtain." Among team "evil" is "Colonel Green." Green speaks with an American accent and is described as leading "a genocidal war early in the twenty-first century on Earth." (The actor that played Colonel Green bore a certain resemblance to the future President George W. Bush—an amazing coincidence!)

CONCLUSION

Brian J. Snee in *Lincoln before Lincoln* elides the treatment of the 16th American president in *Star Trek*, the original series. This is significant because Lincoln's portrayal in "Savage Curtain" is the most important popular culture treatment of Lincoln. Snee holds that prior to Spielberg's *Lincoln*, broadcast iterations of Lincoln underplayed or ignored the view of Lincoln as "Great Emancipator." Thus, Lincoln in both movies and television has not been conveyed as a figure of great historic, worldwide importance. In *Star Trek*, however, Lincoln is cast as a person that shaped Earth's politics, even long into the future.

The creators of Star Trek use the figure of Lincoln to forward a view of world politics that is globalist and post-nationalist. This is suggested in *Star Trek* because Lincoln remains a greatly admired figure in the twenty-third century—when the nation-state system on Earth no longer exists. Additionally, the character of Lincoln plays opposite other world historic figures in the Star Trek universe: Surak of Vulcan and Kahless of the Klingon Empire. Moreover, the character of Colonel Green in "Savage Curtain" indicates that American politics/nationalism (while having its positive features—e.g., Lincoln as Great Emancipator) also has darker, even sinister dimensions.

Star Trek, the original series, makes a broad argument against nationalism—either as manifest in the Cold War of the time or in Nazism. Reflective of how the original series was outside of nationalism and adopted a globalist stance, it provides a sustained critique of American foreign policy in the post–World War II period. Again, Lincoln in *Star Trek* is utilized to make an affirmative argument for globalism and a post-nationalist humanity.

NOTES

1. Brian J. Snee, *Lincoln before Lincoln* (Lexington: University Press of Kentucky, 2016), 25.
2. Ibid., 22.
3. Rick Worland, "Captain Kirk: Cold Warrior," *Journal of Popular Film & Television* 16, no. 3 (1988), 110.
4. Mark Lagon, "'We Owe It to Them to Interfere': Star Trek and U.S. Statecraft in the 1960s and the 1990s," in *Political Science Fiction*, Donald M. Hassler and Clyde Wilcox, ed. (Columbia: University of South Carolina Press, 1997), 235.
5. Keith M. Booker, "The Politics of Star Trek," in *The Essential Science Fiction Reader*, J. P. Telotte, ed. (Lexington: University Press of Kentucky, 2008), 197.
6. George A. Gonzalez, *The Politics of Star Trek: Justice, War, and the Future* (New York: Palgrave Macmillan, 2015).
7. Roland Vegso, *The Naked Communist: Cold War Modernism and the Politics of Popular Culture* (New York: Fordham University Press, 2013). Modernism is a set of normative values that privileges reason and secularism, as opposed to obscurantism and political religion (i.e., theocracy). Peter Childs, *Modernism* (New York: Routledge, 2007).
8. Richard Carwardine and Jay Sexton, eds., *The Global Lincoln* (New York: Oxford University Press, 2011), ix.

9. James M. McPherson, *Abraham Lincoln and the Second American Revolution* (New York: Oxford University Press, 1992); James Oakes *Freedom National: The Destruction of Slavery in the United States* (New York: W. W. Norton & Company, 2012).

10. For example, (*Star Trek*, original series—"All Our Yesterdays" 1969).

11. Yoram Hazony, *The Virtue of Nationalism* (New York: Basic Books, 2018).

12. Daniel Bernardi, *Star Trek and History: Race-ing toward a White Future* (Newark, NJ: Rutgers University Press, 1998).

13. Vegso, *The Naked Communist*.

14. In "Errand of Mercy" (1967—original series) the following exchange takes place between a Klingon commander and Captain Kirk.

Klingon: You of the Federation, you are much like us.

Kirk: We're nothing like you. We're a democratic body.

Klingon: Come now. I'm not referring to minor ideological differences. I mean that we are similar as a species. Here wer are on a planet of sheep. Two tigers, predators, hunters, killers, and it is precisely that which makes us great. And there is a universe to be taken.

15. (*Next Generation*—"Encounter at Farpoint" 1987).

16. Kirk tells the Yangs that the U.S. Constitution "was not written for chiefs or kings or warriors or the rich and powerful, but for all the people!"

17. While Nicholas Evan Sarantakes thoughtfully acknowledges that *Star Trek* cannot be reduced to pro-American propaganda, he, nevertheless, holds that "In episodes involving foreign policy, the Klingons represent the Soviet Union." "Cold War Pop Culture and the Image of U.S. Foreign Policy: The Perspective of the Original Star Trek of U.S. Foreign Policy," *Journal of Cold War Studies* 7, no. 4 (2005), 78.

18. Christian Domenig, "Klingons: Going Medieval on You," in *Star Trek and History*, Nancy R. Reagin, ed. (Hoboken, NJ: John Wiley & Sons, 2013).

19. Jacqueline S. Ismael, *Kuwait: Dependency and Class in a Rentier State* (Gainesville: University of Florida Press, 1993); Giovanni Arrighi, with Beverly Silver, *Chaos and Governance in the Modern World System* (Minneapolis: University of Minnesota Press, 1999); Immanuel Wallerstein, *World-Systems Analysis: An Introduction* (Durham, NC: Duke University Press, 2004); Harold Kerbo, *World Poverty: The Roots of Global Inequality and the Modern World System* (New York: McGraw-Hill, 2005).

20. John Dickie, *Cosa Nostra: A History of the Sicilian Mafia* (New York: Palgrave Macmillan, 2005); Selwyn Raab, *Five Families: The Rise, Decline, and Resurgence of America's Most Powerful Mafia Empires* (New York: St. Martin's Griffin, 2006); Letizia Paoli, *Mafia Brotherhoods: Organized Crime, Italian Style* (New York: Oxford University Press, 2008).

21. Booker, "The Politics of Star Trek," 205–206.

22. Booker, "The Politics of Star Trek," 205–206.

23. Booker, "The Politics of Star Trek," 202–203.

24. Lagon, "'We Owe It to Them to Interfere,'" 246.

25. (*Star Trek*, original series—"A Piece of the Action" 1968).

26. Michael E. Latham, *Modernization as Ideology: American Social Science and "Nation Building" in the Kennedy Era* (Chapel Hill: University of North Carolina Press, 2000); and *The Right Kind of Revolution: Modernization, Development, and U.S. Foreign Policy from the Cold War to the Present* (Ithaca, NY: Cornell University Press, 2010); Nils Gilman, *Mandarins of the Future: Modernization Theory in Cold War America* (Baltimore, MD: Johns Hopkins University Press, 2007).

Chapter Four

The Politics of Race and Class Oppression in Star Trek

The broadcast iterations of the Star Trek text arguable holds the broadest audience in all of popular culture. Thus, it is an important terrain of identity politics—with prominent critics charging that the franchise contains negative ethnic (racial) biases. Star Trek in fact takes a strong and lucid anti-racist stance. Moreover, the franchise indicates that racism is linked to class oppression. In Star Trek's utopian future, class oppression no longer exists.

The Next Generation series, reflecting the resurgent nationalism of the Reagan Revolution,[1] does convey a racialist politics—that is, the idea that nations and cultures are permanently cleaved into discrete entities.[2] This racialist outlook dominates the Star Trek series *Enterprise*. The franchise should be read as both depicting and critiquing racialist thinking.

Star Trek and Race

Daniel Bernardi in his book on race and the Star Trek franchise takes issue with the fact that the character of Lt. Uhuru (of the original series—played by an Afro actor) was limited to a supporting role in the original series.[3] André M. Carrington in *Speculative Blackness: The Future of Race in Science Fiction* takes a similarly negative tone with Uhuru's role on Star Trek as mostly a supporting character: "In light of the possibility for exterior adventures, the confinement of [Uhura] to the bridge relegated her diversifying function to a 'domestic' sphere, leaving her 'home' while adventures 'away' remained the province of the series's male leads."[4] The fact that the show was mostly centered on the characters of Kirk, Spock, and McCoy amounts to nothing more than artistic choices, and efforts to identify sinister motives in these choices is entirely cynical as well as misplaced.

The presence of Uhura and other actors with Afro backgrounds on the original Star Trek are noteworthy (because as Carrington notes elsewhere in his book), racism in the science fiction genre has historically been manifest by denying the existence of people of color. That Uhura had a minimal role in the show's plots is neither here nor there—as a true racist stance would never afford a bridge officer position to an African American. Also noteworthy is the fact that an African-American actor (in the original series) plays one of the Federation's leading scientific minds.[5]

Bernardi's and Carrington's treatment of Uhura is significant in that their criticisms are at cross purposes. Bernardi faults the Star Trek franchise because it represents "a Western and white standard."[6] Yet when Uhura's quarters in "The Tholian Web" (1968—original series) have African-theme accouterments (featuring, for instance, a zebra skin bed spread) Carrington denounces this because he holds it equates people with an Afro background with "primitivism."[7] It is unclear how the likes of Bernardi or Carrington expect Afro peoples on the Enterprise to behave.

Perhaps what is most glaring in Bernardi's and Carrington's treatment of the identity politics of the Star Trek franchise is the fact that neither make any comment on the original series episode "Let That Be Your Last Battlefield" (1969)—an episode that is explicitly anti-racist. The Enterprise crew comes into contact with an alien race that is half white and half black, but part of the population is white on the right side and the other is white on the left side. The Enterprise crew cannot fathom that such a trivial difference would be politically and socially significant for anyone—much less fuel the intense hatred and violence that the two alien individuals on board the Enterprise direct toward one another (each one from the different ethnic groups). In the end we learn that the racism of this species resulted in its destruction.

It is significant that in the denouement of the episode, Uhura proclaims that the behavior of these aliens "doesn't make any sense." She resides in a world of ethnic equality and fairness and cannot understand how people could hate so profoundly over something like skin tone—of course, viewers in the 1960s could. Spock, a Vulcan who works among humans, is similarly incredulous: "To expect sense from two mentalities of such extreme viewpoints is not logical."

Returning to the issue of expunging or ignoring the existence of Afro people in science fiction, if we take this as a marker of racism, then Bernardi's 1998 book qualifies. The title of Bernardi's book is *Star Trek and History: Race-ing toward a White Future*. Despite having such a title, Bernardi in his book, rather amazingly, fails to discuss *Deep Space Nine*—which had an African-American captain and had been running for five years before the publication of his book (1998).

Carrington notes that "though it was on the air at the time of [Bernardi's] publication, [Bernardi] omits any substantive discussion of the significance of *Deep Space Nine*."[8] Interestingly, this does not stop Carrington from praising him: "Bernardi's work ably explains how the original *Star Trek* and *The Next Generation* envision a future beyond racism while still falling prey to the shortcomings of the liberal discourse that produced them."[9] Bernardi minimizes the character of Uhura (as noted above). Additionally, Bernardi minimizes *The Next Generation* characters of Geordi Laforge, Worf, and Guinan (all played by African-American actors). Elsewhere, I hold that "these characters are admirable—of the highest intelligence, fortitude, and integrity."[10] Carrington doesn't bother to discuss them.

Empire and Racism

Carrington makes the following unfounded claim: "Star Trek is a discovery narrative, imaging a new age of exploration modeled on European colonial expeditions."[11] As I explain in chapter 3, original series episodes are perhaps the most powerful and clear-throated critiques of empire and colonialism in all of popular culture: "Mirror, Mirror" (1967), "Arena" (1967), "Private Little War" (1968), "A Piece of the Action" (1968), "The Paradise Syndrome" (1968), "Patterns of Force"(1968), and "Friday's Child" (1967). All these episodes to one degree or another take aim at colonialism and empire. As an anti-imperialist tract, "Mirror, Mirror" is particularly noteworthy.

Carrington's use of the phrase "European colonial expeditions" is on its face racist. Firstly, in world history Europeans were certainly not the only peoples to engage in colonialism. Hence, Carrington vilifies Europeans as the only ones guilty of the sins of colonialism. Secondly, Carrington's description of the Star Trek text as based on "a new age of exploration modeled on European colonial expeditions" can be read as marginalizing people of color's role in Star Trek's narrative "to go where no one has gone before." This is a European affair and people of color are only pawns in this project. This casts the characters of Uhura, Geordi, Worf, and so on, in a subservient and demeaning light.

Class and Racism

What is most significant and important about Star Trek's anti-racism is that its creators seek to identify the causes of institutional racism. Racism is a function of class oppression. In the *Deep Space Nine* episode "Far Beyond the Stars" (1998), Captain Sisko is transported back in time—to New York City in the 1950s, where he is a staff writer for a science fiction magazine. African Americans are publicly denied any space in the genre during this time, and Sisko's personae (Benny Russell) is asked not to show up to work the day the magazine is set to take the staff picture (as is the sole woman writer on staff). Sisko/Russell gets inspired to write the story of the Deep

Space Nine station, along with its African-American captain. Very importantly, the entirety of the staff, along with the managing editor, support Russell and press to have his story published. In the end, the (unseen) owner of the magazine decides to "pulp" the issue that month. It is made clear that he would rather lose the money than distribute a story featuring a black character. In the original series episode "Patterns of Force," the argument is made that racism is a tool used by elites to maintain societal stability: "Why do the Nazis hate Zeons?" "Because without us to hate, there'd be nothing to hold them together." The "Day of the Dove" (1968—original series) has an alien forcing the crew of the Enterprise to engage in "race hatred." "Plato's Stepchildren" (1968—original series) casts a planet's powerful elites as sadists who enjoy inflicting sexual and physical abuse. Viewers see Uhura forced into kissing someone and threatened with a whip.

The original series episode "Cloud Minders"(1969) depicts a society (the planet of Ardana) where torture technology ("the rays")—and racism—are used to maintain/stabilize a caste system. (Ardana is a seeming stand-in for South Africa.) In effective imagery the political/economic/social realities of the planet are portrayed—with the privileged/governing caste living a life of aesthetic splendor in a "cloud city" ("Stratos") floating in the heavens; on the (barren) planet surface are where the laboring classes (referred to as "Troglytes") live—working the mines (extracting "zenite"). The residents of Stratos are fair-skinned and fair-haired and partake in the high arts. The Troglytes are dark-haired, dark-skinned, and unwashed.

"The rays" are deployed in an effort to break a political movement in opposition to the governing regime. A prisoner is pressed to provide the names of the putative leaders of the mining caste's rebellion: "You still refuse to disclose the names of the other Disrupters." "There are no Disrupters!" "Very well, if you prefer the rays." She screams in agony, discomforting onlookers. Spock, in his famous, calm, and equanimous voice, observes that "violence in reality is quite different from theory."

> Plausus (a resident of Stratos): But what else can [Troglytes] understand, Mister Spock?

> Spock: All the little things you and I understand and expect from life, such as equality, kindness, justice.

> Plausus: Troglytes are not like Stratos dwellers, Mister Spock. They're a conglomerate of inferior species.

As noted in chapter 1, Star Trek makes clear that in the future, class oppression for humans and Earth is no longer an issue. Beginning in the late 1980s Star Trek starts to base its plots on racialist thinking. The original series was produced in the aftermath of the international solidarity in the fight against fascism and during the social justice politics of the New Deal and the Great Society. Later Star Trek was produced during the politically conservative Reagan Revolution, when cynicism set in about social justice and nationalism was resurgent. Later Star Trek both conveys and critiques the racialist thinking that became predominant as part of the Reagan Revolution.

Racialist Ideation in Star Trek

Star Trek is notable and laudable for its treatment and denunciation of racism. Beginning with Star Trek of the late 1980s, nevertheless, the franchise shifts to what can be labeled racialist reasoning. In other words, that there are insurmountable, even genetic, differences between cultures. In "The Icarus Factor" (1989—*Next Generation*) the point is explicitly made by the steadfastly objective Lt. Comdr. Data that "there is, of course, a genetic predisposition toward hostility among all Klingons." The Romulans in the *Next Generation* are cast in broad-brushed racialist terms as "violent beyond description"; also "their belief in their own superiority is beyond arrogance."[12] While the galaxy of Star Trek in the 1980s is permanently cleaved into different racialist societies (the Romulans, the Klingons, the Cardassians, and so on), there are no specific claims of racial superiority. All these cultures are the technological equal of the Federation—the quintessential modernist society.

Nevertheless, Star Trek does indicate that racialism does result in xenophobia. The xenophobia of the Klingons is evident when Worf is chided for bringing "*outsiders* [i.e., humans] to our Great Hall."[13] In another instance, one Klingon is opposed to another Klingon marrying a non-Klingon: "She believes that by bringing aliens into our families we risk losing our identity as Klingons." This is acknowledged as "a prejudiced, xenophobic view."[14]

The racism in racialist reasoning is particularly evident in the *Next Generation* episode "Birthright" (1993). The action centers on a prison camp established by the Romulans over twenty years earlier to house a group of Klingons who could not return home. They were stigmatized by the fact that they were taken prisoner—Klingons are expected to fight to the death or commit suicide if captured. As an act of kindness, and at great sacrifice, a Romulan officer agrees to oversee the camp—otherwise the captured Klingons would be executed. Worf—whose father was falsely rumored to be at the camp—discovers it. He objects to an arrangement whereby Klingons live as prisoners of the Romulans—even though they are treated well, have complete freedom on the planet they reside on, have given birth to children, and share a strong sense of community. Worf, nevertheless, tells the Romulan camp commander (Tokath) that "you robbed the Klingons of who they were. *You dishonored them.*" Tokath, pointing to the irrationality of Worf's position, retorts, "By not slitting their throats when we found them unconscious?" Worf explicitly resorts to racialist thinking to justify his position: "I do not expect you to understand. *You are a Romulan.*" Hence, there is something *particular* about Klingons, and it is inscrutable to non-Klingons. Tokath explains "We've put aside the old hatreds. Here, Romulans and Klingons live in peace." Worf is unmoved: "Do not deceive yourself. These people are not happy here. I see the sadness in their eyes."

Worf adopts an openly hateful attitude when he comes to discover that a woman (Ba'el) he is romantically interested in is an offspring of one of the Klingon prisoners and a Romulan. Worf is kissing Ba'el, draws back her hair and sees her pointed ears (characteristic of Romulans). Outraged Worf exclaims "You are Romulan!" Unabashed in his racism, he asks with a tone of disgust: "How could your mother mate with a Romulan?" He declares, "It is an obscenity!" Fully venting his racism, Worf tells Ba'el, "Romulans are treacherous, deceitful. They are without honor." Ba'el: "My father is a good man. He is kind, and generous. There is nothing dishonorable about him."

Earth-Vulcan Relations in *Enterprise*

Racialist reasoning is at the core of the Star Trek television series, *Enterprise*. Perhaps the most salient aspect of the *Enterprise* narrative is that unlike in the original series where the Vulcans and Earthlings are part of the same Federation polity, in this series Earth and Vulcan have an uneasy relationship and form two discrete political formations. *Enterprise* indicates that with racialism as politically dominant this propels Earthlings toward xenophobia. Additionally, as seen through the Xindi (described below) racialism in the modern era can lead to planetary destruction.

It is significant that in the movie script of *Star Trek: First Contact* (1996) by 2063 San Francisco is destroyed.[15] As noted above, in "Past Tense" (1995—*Deep Space Nine*), San Francisco is where the *anti-neoliberalist* Bell Uprising occurs in 2024 (i.e., the basis of a new global politics). *Star Trek: First Contact* is predicated on a WE/THEY distinction. The action of the movie takes place in the year 2063. The Borg go back in Earth's history to prevent humanity's first contact with the Vulcans. This initial exposure to an alien culture occurs because Zephran Cochrane conducts humanity's first successful warp drive experiment. ("Warp speed" represents a speed faster than light.) When the Vulcans detect Cochrane's ship achieving warp speed they decide to introduce themselves to earthlings—"first contact." In this iteration (*First Contact*) of Star Trek's historiography of Earth in 2063, humanity is in what is referred to in the movie script notes as a "Second Dark Age."[16] What rallies humanity from its disarray is its contact with the Vulcans: "*It unites humanity in a way no one ever thought possible when they realize they're not alone in the universe.*" This is consonant with Samuel Huntington's racialist *clash of civilizations* argument, where he holds that "for peoples seeking identity and reinventing ethnicity, *enemies are essential.*"[17]

Therefore, the political foundation of humanity in the mid-twenty-first century is the WE/THEY dichotomy—with the Vulcans serving as "They"—and this is the basis of *Enterprise* (set in the twenty-second century, whereas the original series is set in the twenty-third century and *Next Generation, Deep Space Nine, Voyager*, and *Discovery* [2017 to present] in the twenty-fourth century). In *Enterprise* conflict/competition with the Vulcans does occur. "The Forge" (2004), "Awakening" (2004), and the "Kir'Shara" (2004) is a three-episode story arc whereby Earth's embassy on Vulcan is bombed, killing Admiral Forrest (Captain Archer's mentor), and the Enterprise crew gets swept up in internal Vulcan religious and political strife—with an effort made against Captain Archer's life and the Enterprise and Vulcan military ships coming to a face-off. In the denouement we learn that elements within the Vulcan government were behind the bombing of the Earth embassy, and that a faction still in the government wants to pull the planet toward a political/military alliance with the Romulans. An intention ominously threatening to Earth as it suggests the formation of a Vulcan-Romulan civilization (they are the same ethnicity).

Especially telling for a politics based on competing *civilizations*, *Enterprise* conveys Earth's polity as afflicted with xenophobia and racism. The series concludes in 2005 and the penultimate episode centers on the group "Terra Prime" (episode title). Initially, this organization is described as xenophobic: "They want to stop all contact with alien species." "They believe it's corrupting our way of life." Later, we learn that Terra Prime is racist: "This is an alien-human hybrid. Living proof of what will happen if we allow ourselves to be submerged in an interstellar coalition. Our genetic heritage . . ." "That child is a cross-breed freak. How many generations before our genome is so diluted that the word human is nothing more than a footnote in some medical text?" The leader of Terra Prime declares, "I'm returning Earth to its rightful owners." Referring to signs of broad sympathy for Terra Prime and its agenda, the Vulcan Ambassador Soval notes, "The fact that [Terra Prime] has the support of so many of your people is . . . troubling."

Of great significance for a discussion based on Huntington's vision of world politics informed by the idea of conflictive *civilizations* is the Xindi—introduced in *Enterprise*. The Xindi are the former inhabitants of the planet Xindi. The Xindi are cleaved into five distinct *civilizations* with each civilization corresponding to a distinct species: insectoid, humanoid, aquatic, ape-like, and reptilian. As a result of their competition, the Xindi destroyed their planet: "The war went on for nearly a hundred years. . . . The insectoids and reptilians detonated massive explosions beneath the eight largest seismic fissures. I'd like to think they didn't realize how devastating the result would be."[18]

CONCLUSION

As arguably the most popular and politically modern text in the world, the Star Trek franchise (its broadcast iterations) serves as a saliently important political theory corpus. Critics of this corpus hold that it depicts negative ethnic biases. Such criticisms are without merit, as the Star Trek text is explicitly anti-racist. An innovation for a popular culture medium, Star Trek links racism and class oppression. The utopia of Star Trek eliminates class and racism.

Star Trek of the late 1980s adopts the racialism of the Reagan Revolution, with the Star Trek series, *Enterprise*, explicitly predicated on racialist politics. In depicting this racialism Star Trek offers key critiques of racialist politics—namely, that such politics result in xenophobia. Significantly, Star Trek (through the parable of the Xindi) indicates that racialism can result in planetary destruction in the modern era.

NOTES

1. Doug Rossinow, *The Reagan Era: A History of the 1980s* (New York: Columbia University Press, 2015).
2. Samuel P. Huntington, *The Clash of Civilizations and the Remaking of World Order* (New York: Simon & Schuster, 1996 [2011]).
3. Daniel Leonard Bernardi, *Star Trek and History: Race-ing toward a White Future* (New Brunswick, NJ: Rutgers University Press, 1998).
4. André M. Carrington, *Speculative Blackness: The Future of Race in Science Fiction* (Minneapolis: University of Minnesota Press, 2016), 73–74.
5. (*Star Trek*, original series—"The Ultimate Computer" 1968).
6. Bernardi, *Star Trek and History*, 130.
7. Carrington, *Speculative Blackness*, 74
8. Carrington, *Speculative Blackness*, 160.
9. Ibid.
10. George A. Gonzalez, *The Politics of Star Trek: Justice, War, and the Future* (New York: Palgrave Macmillan, 2015), 2.
11. Carrington, *Speculative Blackness*, 161.
12. (*Next Generation*—"The Neutral Zone" 1988).
13. (*Next Generation*—"Sins of the Father" 1990).
14. (*Deep Space Nine*—"You Are Cordially Invited" 1997).
15. The following is in the 1995 movie script:

Scrimm (2063 resident of Earth): "Where are you from most recently?"

Picard: "California. San Francisco"

Scrimm: "Beautiful city. Used to be, anyway. I didn't think anyone still lived there.

http://www.st-minutiae.com/academy/literature329/fc.txt
16. http://www.st-minutiae.com/academy/literature329/fc.txt
17. Huntington, *The Clash of Civilizations and the Remaking of World Order*, 20, emphasis added.
18. (*Enterprise*—"The Shipment" 2003).

Chapter Five

Popular Culture on Good, Evil, and Post-Traumatic Stress Disorder

The Devil in the television series *Lucifer* (2016 to present) holds that he's not evil, but in fact a deterrent to evil. Lucifer Morningstar (the Devil's alter ego) declares, "I'm not evil. I punish evil" ("#TeamLucifer" 2016). Indeed, in (Biblical) mythology the Devil is seemingly not the cause of evil but a warning against committing evil—overseeing Hell. At worst, the Devil tempts people into evil (the most famous example being Eve). In holding that the devil is not evil incarnate, the television series *Lucifer* is making an important metaphysical claim: evil is not a metaphysical entity.[1] Of course, analytic philosophers hold that neither good nor evil metaphysically exists. Good and evil amount to only personal subjective judgements. Put differently, there are no objectively good or evil acts.[2]

The Star Trek franchise, contrary to the thinking that predominates among analytic philosophers, indicates that good exists. Good is manifest in the progressive dialectic—first identified by Karl Marx. The progressive dialectic is deduced from the Hegalian absolute.[3] The failure to pursue the progressive dialectic, according to the Star Trek text, results in societal collapse. Thus, there is the good of the Absolute (as manifest in the progressive dialectic), and the failure to pursue this dialectic to its full fruition leads to a horrible, bad outcome—dystopia. Again, like in *Lucifer*, there is no evil, only actions against the good (i.e., the progressive dialectic).

The documentary *Of Men and War* (2014) provides important additional insight into the question of good and evil. The documentary focuses on the issue of post-traumatic stress disorder (PTSD). The condition of PTSD indicates that murderous acts against the progressive dialectic impose debilitating damage on the human mind. Both PTSD and the existence of the human mind both indicate that the *material realism* of analytic philosophy is invalid.

Chapter 5
"BAD" VERSUS "GOOD" WARS

Star Trek presents an argument as to what is good—the progressive dialectic, and forwarding that dialectic is to do good. What does this mean for the individual and judging his or her actions? PTSD should be read as evidence that acting against the progressive dialectic is bad or even evil. PTSD (in one form or another) has been portrayed in American popular culture since the late-1970s—with movies about the experiences of American soldiers who have returned from the Vietnam War.

Movies like *Deerhunter* (1978), *First Blood* (1982), and *Born on the 4th of July* (1989) point to the psychological damage of soldiers resulting from their experiences in the Vietnam War.[4] The dramatized emotional damage of these characters arguably stems from the fact that the Vietnam War struck against the progressive dialectic. While American cinema beginning in the late 1970s suggested that the Vietnam War was a blow against the progressive dialectic (as described below), Star Trek in the 1990s depicts a just war.

The last two seasons of *Deep Space Nine* are mostly dedicated to the Dominion War. The Dominion seeks to conquer the Federation (the interstellar institution led by Earth) because "many years ago we set ourselves the task of imposing order on a chaotic universe" (*Deep Space Nine*—"The Search" 1994). The leaders of the Dominion, the Founders (who oversee a massive military), are cast as ruthless and place no value whatsoever on the lives of humanoids. (The Founders' natural state is one of liquid.) In one noteworthy scene a Founder decides that a new set of Vorta humanoids should be brought in to research a cure for the affliction she is suffering from. The Founder is informed a "team of Vorta Doctors [is] working night and day to find a cure." The Founder orders, "Have them document their efforts. *Then eliminate them*." "Founder?" her Vorta aide asks. She explains, "Activate their clones and order them to continue their predecessors' work. Perhaps a fresh perspective will speed matters along."[5]

In the face of the mortal threat that the Federation confronts with the Dominion, the Federation can undertake actions that would not be allowed in peacetime. Particularly significant on this score is "Inter Arma Enim Silent Leges" (1999—*Deep Space Nine*). Deep Space Nine's Doctor Bashir is used as a pawn in a game of intrigue that politically destroys a would-be ally, a Romulan Sentor Cretak. Bashir confronts Admiral Ross (who oversaw the operation):

> Bashir: And what about your "friend" Senator Cretak? What will happen to her?
> Ross: Dismissed from the [Romulan] Senate—definitely. Imprisoned—most likely.
> Bashir: Executed?
> Ross: I hope not.

When Bashir challenges Ross over the ethical, moral, and legal ramifications of the compromising of Senator Cretak, Ross responds in Latin: "Inter arma enim silent leges"—"*In time of war, the laws fall silent.*"

According to Star Trek, war does allow a *federation* to pursue the enemy outside of home territory—that is, attacking foes on their territory (an offensive military campaign). In the penultimate episode of *Deep Space Nine* ("The Dogs of War" 1999), the Federation takes the upper hand, as the Dominion retreats from enemy space and adopts a defensive posture. The Federation military leadership reason the Dominion's defensive posture is purely intended as an effort to regroup and rebuild its military capabilities for further war.[6] The alliance musters its forces to defeat the Dominion.

After a major space battle, the Dominion is defeated and falls back to its last bastion, the Cardassian home world. Even though it has been defeated, the Dominion retains considerable military resources deployed around Cardassia. The point is made that the Dominion could be "bottled up . . . indefinitely." Nevertheless, the Federation military leadership decides to conquer the last bastion of the Dominion.[7]

If the tactics of *empire* and *federation* are no different in the context of war, how does a solider for the *federation* know they are fighting for protection/defense and not for *empire*—that is, conquest and control? Star Trek presumes a commitment to the truth among the military/political leaders of *federation* to ensure tactics pursued during war are not used to dupe their populace (and soldiers). This is in sharp contrast to the leaders of *empire*. In pursuing the invasion of Cardassia and thereby ending the decades old Klingon-Federation alliance, the Klingon Empire head of government, Chancellor Gowron, declares that "*history is written by the victors*" (*Deep Space Nine*—"The Way of the Warrior" 1995). Contrary to this sentiment that the perception of reality (facts) is malleable and can/should be shaped to serve any (corrupt) agenda, Captain Picard declares that "the first duty of every Starfleet officer is to the *truth*. Whether it's scientific truth, or historical truth, or personal truth. *It is the guiding principle upon which Starfleet is based*" (*Next Generation*—"The First Duty" 1992). In another instance, Picard, speaking to one of the leading political figures of the Federation ("Sarek"—1992), declares, "Sarek of Vulcan never confused what he wanted with the *truth*" (*Next Generation*).

Star Trek indicates that in the context of *federation*, the public can trust its leaders. *Deep Space Nine* episode "Paradise Lost" (1996) makes this specific claim. When Captain Sisko comes to understand that his commanding officer is conspiring against the government of Earth, Sisko, along with other officers subordinate to the conspirator, reject the chain of command and thwart the conspiracy. Similarly, when the crew of the Federation starship "Pegasus" (episode title—1994) realized that their captain was engaging in illegal research into cloaking technology, they mutinied *(Next Genera-*

tion). Additionally, in the movie *Insurrection* (1998), once Picard et al. from the Enterprise learn that the Federation leadership has sanctioned the forced removal of a village, they directly block this removal. Similarly, in the 2013 Star Trek movie *Into Darkness*, when the Enterprise crew learn that elements within Starfleet conducted a false-flag operation to initiate a war with the Klingons, Kirk et al. successfully expose the subterfuge. Therefore, the embedded institutional commitment to (or ethics of) *truth* (morality; legality; fairness) in Starfleet (Federation institutions) serves as an effective prophylactic to conspiracies to bamboozle the public (soldiers). As Picard informed Data, "Starfleet doesn't want officers who will blindly follow orders without analyzing the situation" ("Redemption" 1991—*Next Generation*).

Star Trek makes the further claim that a prime duty of military officers' (political leaders') within *federation* is to prevent authoritarian outcomes. The *Deep Space Nine* episode "Past Tense" (1995) features the following exchange between Dr. Julian Bashir and Captain Sisko:

> Are humans really any different than Cardassians . . . or Romulans? If push came to shove, if something disastrous happened to the Federation, and we got frightened enough, or desperate enough, how would we react? Would we stay true to our ideals . . . or would we just [resort to authoritarian/oppressive means]?

Captain Sisko responds "I don't know. But as a Starfleet officer, it's my job to make sure we never have to find out."

POST-TRAUMATIC STRESS DISORDER

This can explain the wounded warrior movie genre—American soldiers who fought in Vietnam and Iraq think their leaders deceived them. American leaders argued that the U.S. military role in Vietnam was necessary to protect against the Soviet Union. American cinema of the 1970s and 1980s suggests otherwise. Similarly, the George W. Bush administration falsely claimed that the Iraqi Saddam Hussein regime had weapons of mass destruction that could be used against the United States. In the case of the Afghanistan War (2001 to present), the American military invaded for the stated reason of capturing the perpetrators of the 9/11 attacks. Ron Kovic in *Born on the July of 4th* comes to believe that false patriotism was used to entice soldiers (including himself) to fight in Vietnam. The movie *No Escape* (1994) features a character that killed his commanding general because the general's duplicity resulted in the soldier massacring scores of innocent people. The *Green Zone* (2010) documents the failure to find weapons of mass destruction in Iraq after the 2003 invasion.

Thus, American soldiers believe they killed, were injured (often permanently), and their comrades were killed not to forward or protect the progressive dialectic. Instead of fighting for the progressive dialectic, perhaps soldiers in Vietnam et al. fought for empire. Empire is seemingly the opposite of the progressive dialectic—as it is the negation of the political equality that is the foundation of the dialectic. Hence, American soldiers conceivably participated in a project of evil—that is, one that directly undermines the progressive dialectic.

PTSD is the specific focus of the documentary *Of Men and War* (2014). The makers of the documentary observe for an extended period of time a set of soldiers who suffer from PTSD. The documentary depicts a number of the therapy sessions that the former soldiers undergo. In these sessions they recount events where they killed. They fixate on these memories to such a degree that they cannot function in life or even live with their families. They all reside in a convalescent home for people with PTSD.

What is particularly noteworthy is that neither the soldiers nor therapists appeal to the normative justifications of the wars they participated in to find solace. Put differently, one can readily imagine a soldier who fought in World War II who suffered from PTSD being told that the death and violence they participated in and witnessed was wholly necessary to defeat the nefarious, dastardly Axis forces (á la the Dominion). When one subject *Of Men and War* discusses being haunted by his memory of killing someone in battle, the therapist justifies this killing by pointing to the fact that the soldier had to kill in order to protect himself. It is easy to understand how this fact would not comfort the PTSD sufferer as the American military should not have been "in country." Were it not for the project against the progressive dialectic this dead individual would presumably be alive. In the *Star Trek: Voyager* episode "Memorial" (2000) members of the Voyager crew suffer from "post-traumatic stress syndrome" as a result of implanted memories. As they discuss their shared memories of killing villagers who violently resisted being relocated, one declares, "We had no right to be there!"

PTSD AND THE METAPHYSICS OF MEMORY

PTSD is an affliction of the mind and memory.[8] Materialist (or analytic philosophy) conceptions of the mind are of little use when one considers Noam Chomsky's theory of memory and innate language. Chomsky takes note of the fact that children learn languages and concepts with incredible speed. From this, Chomsky reasons that humans have to be born with innate (memory) language skills/concepts.[9] Analytic philosophers take this conclusion to support the position that language is a process where we attach words to concepts/pictures in our minds.[10] For this argument to be viable, one must adopt a strong theological position—namely, that some deity ("The Great Programmer") wrote all concepts into the human mind from the beginning. Pictures/images of all things had to embedded in the brain from the inception of humanity, simply awaiting their invention/creation. Presumably, there are pictures in our minds of future inventions/creations. When finally produced, we will readily recognize them and quickly adopt words to refer to them.

An argument not explicitly rooted in theology, is a theory of memory and language relying on the existence of the absolute. As humans create knowledge, this knowledge is accumulated in the absolute. Future generations access/remember this knowledge. This is where the matter of PTSD arguably arises—former soldiers find it difficult/impossible to accept that their egregious crimes against the progressive dialectic will live for time immemorial in the Absolute. In the *Voyager* episode "Memorial," the Voyager crew confront and cope with the pain of their memories by embracing them. They decide that the machine that implanted the memories of the atrocities be repaired so others can "remember" this enormity.

Star Trek demonstrates that humans are creatures of history/memory. People intuitively refer to history in judging/analyzing their own politics and societies. When a political witch hunt erupts on the Enterprise, Picard is steeled in his opposition to the hysteria by his knowledge of history:

> Five hundred years ago, military officers would upend a drum on the battlefield, sit at it and dispense summary justice. Decisions were quick, punishments severe, appeals denied. Those who came to a drumhead were doomed. (*Next Generation*—"The Drumhead" 1991)

More broadly, in the *Next Generation* pilot ("Farpoint Station" 1987) when Q condemns humanity based on its violent history, Picard objects, arguing that humanity is well aware of this history and is determined not to repeat it. (Picard: "That nonsense is centuries behind us!" "Even as far back as . . . we had begun to make rapid progress.") Thus, consistent with a theory that indicates that knowledge of the past is accumulated in the absolute that in turn is manifest in children's intellectual prodigiousness, is the fact that humans regularly refer to history to understand/comprehend the present. Thus, human consciousness is figuratively a product of history/memory, and in all likelihood is literally one *vis-à-vis* the absolute.

CONCLUSION

Relying on popular culture I have posited a theory of good and evil. Drawing from the Star Trek franchise, good is determined by the Absolute as manifest in the progressive dialectic—where the end goal is robust political equality. Good actions are those that positively contribute to the progressive dialectic.

Evil, or the normatively bad, are actions that undermine the progressive dialectic. Thus, as the creators of *Lucifer* suggest, evil is not a thing but actions that can be judged egregiously bad *vis-à-vis* the progressive dialectic.

Thus, we can judge war and killing according to the criteria of whether or not such actions contribute to the progressive dialectic. Worse case scenario, such actions contribute to empire—a political circumstance where political domination and economic exploitation are the norm (the opposite of the progressive dialectic). PTSD is a condition that results from acting egregiously (e.g., killing) for a purpose that is neutral or actually contrary to the progressive dialectic. The idea that these actions are indelibly marked in the Absolute is too much to bear for the suffers of PTSD. Conversely, the Star Trek franchise depicts the Dominion War (a just war) where killing is justified and even morally necessary. Such violence and killing is necessary to protect the progressive dialectic—or a society predicated on the progressive dialectic (as is putatively the Federation)—from a destructive, mortal threat.

NOTES

1. Russ Shafer-Landau, *Whatever Happened to Good and Evil?* (New York: Oxford University Press, 2003); Ronald E. Osborn, *Humanism and the Death of God: Searching for the Good after Darwin, Marx, and Nietzsche* (Oxford University Press, 2017).

2. Hans-Johann Glock, *What is Analytic Philosophy?* (New York: Cambridge University Press, 2008); Stephen P. Schwartz, *A Brief History of Analytic Philosophy: From Russell to Rawls* (West Sussex, UK: Wiley-Blackwell, 2012); Jan Westerhoff, *Reality: A Very Short Introduction* (New York: Oxford University Press, 2012).

3. Donald Phillip Verene, *Hegel's Absolute: An Introduction to Reading the Phenomenology of Spirit* (Albany: State University New York Press, 2007); Stephen Houlgate, *Hegel's "Phenomenology of Spirit": A Reader's Guide* (New York: Bloomsbury Academic, 2013); Brady Bowman, *Hegel and the Metaphysics of Absolute Negativity* (Cambridge: Cambridge University Press, 2015).

4. Michael Anderegg, ed., *Inventing Vietnam: The War in Film and Television* (Philadelphia: Temple University Press, 1991).

5. (*Deep Space Nine*—"Penumbra" 1999).

6. When it is suggested that "the wiser course would be to simply contain them within their perimeter," Sisko retorts, "That's what they're hoping we'll do—so they'll have time to rebuild their forces" (*Deep Space Nine*—"The Dogs of War" 1999).

7. In the last instance, Odo is able to convince the Dominion leader to surrender, and the final conquest does not take place (*Deep Space Nine*—"That You Leave Behind" 1999).

8. Robert F. Worth, "Aftershock," *New York Times Magazine*, June 12, 2016, MM28.

9. James McGilvray, *Chomsky: Language, Mind, and Politics* (Cambridge: Polity, 1999); Noam Chomsky, *Language and Mind*, 3rd ed. (New York: Cambridge University Press, 2006).

10. Schwartz, *A Brief History of Analytic Philosophy*, 182.

Chapter Six

Clones and the Politics of the Mind in Star Wars and Star Trek

Derek R. Sweet in *Star Wars in the Public Square* creatively uses the Cartoon Network/Netflix animated series *The Clone Wars* to adjudicate/mediate the debate surrounding human cloning.[1] To opponents of human cloning, such cloning calls into question the autonomy of humans—as concerns persist that clones will inherently lack independence or their own distinct personalities. Others indicate that creating human clones is ontologically no different from creating children in the traditional manner. Relying on *The Clone Wars*, Sweet holds that clones are essentially no different from other forms of sentient life. Clones have beliefs and values of their own, act autonomously when necessary, and form familial-like bonds, as well as engage in meaningful friendships and social solidarity.[2] To the extent that the clones in *The Clone Wars* submit to authority and obediently follow orders, it is the result of regimentation and institutional discipline—not because of the cloning process or any specific genetic manipulation.

While basing a television series on characters that are mindless and completely subservient automatons is inherently uninteresting and artistically unviable, there are philosophically more profound reasons why we can expect human clones to essentially be average, run of the mill humans. Firstly, to be a sentient, intelligent being is to be a normative creature. Put differently, to be sentient is to view the world normatively and make normative decisions. Such decisions cannot be preordained—genetically or otherwise. Secondly, the notion that human clones would lack autonomy implies that their politics and values could be genetically programmed. More specifically, that a particular political framework could be genetically programmed into clones. Again, this is beyond credulity.

While Sweet invokes the clone soldiers of the Star Wars franchise, I treat the cloned Jemh'dar soldiers of the Star Trek franchise to develop my arguments concerning the cognitive capacities inherent to sentient life—clones or otherwise. The broadcast iterations of the Star Trek franchise indicate that sentience results from a direct connection to the (normative) reasons of the Absolute, as philosophized by Georg Hegel.[3] Hence, to be sentient is to see the world through the normative lenses of the Absolute. This is evident in Star Trek through the way Geordi LaForge (who has vision with the aid of a prosthetic device) and the android Data comprehend the world around them.

PHILOSOPHY OF THE HUMAN MIND

Lt. Cmdr. Geordi LaForge is the chief engineer for the Enterprise in the *Next Generation* television series. LaForge was born blind, but he sees with aid of a prosthetic device that allows him to see "much of the EM spectrum ranging from simple heat and infrared through radio waves."[4] During the episode "Heart of Glory" (1988—*Next Generation*) the audience and the Enterprise crew are shown how LaForge actually sees the world. Picard describes what LaForge sees as "an undefined form, standing in a visual frenzy." He asks LaForge: "Can you filter out the extraneous information?" LaForge, "No, I get it all simultaneously." Picard: "But it's just a jumble."

Picard: How can you make head or tail of it?

Laforge: I select what I want and then disregard the rest.

LaForge, like the rest of us, knows what to focus on to make sense of the physical world. It's an intuitive process. Thus, like for LaForge, the world is a jumble of light and forms for those of us that have sight, but, yet, we know how to identify a chair, a tree, or another person (for example). Just like LaForge we "select" what we want and "then disregard the rest." LaForge, in another episode, indicates that his vision is limited insofar as it prevents him from seeing as well (normatively) as those that have regular sight: "I want to see in shallow, dim, beautiful human ways. . . . It's not fair. . . . I've never seen a rainbow, sunset, sunrise" (*Next Generation*—"The Naked Now" 1987).

LT. CMDR. DATA AND NORMATIVE VALUES

While LaForge sees the world normatively like the rest of us, Lt. Cmdr. Data is fully able to engage in normative reasoning and fully capable of acting on that reasoning. This is saliently apparent in the episode "The Measure of a

Man" (1989—*Next Generation*). A trial is being held to determine if Data, an android, can resign from Starfleet. The trial hinges on whether or not Data is sentient—that is, a person. To support Data's claim that he is sentient, Captain Picard, who is serving as his advocate, points to Data's normative values:

Picard: What are these?

Data: My [military service] medals.

Picard: Why do you pack them? What logical purpose do they serve?

Data: I do not know, sir. I suppose none. I just wanted them. Is that vanity?

Picard: And this? (Pointing to a book of Data's)

Data: A gift from you, sir.

Picard: You value it?

Data: Yes, sir.

Picard: Why?

Data: It is a reminder of friendship and service.

(Picard activates a hologram of Tasha Yar—a deceased crew member)

Picard: And this? You have no other portraits of your fellow crew members. Why this person?

Data: She was special to me, sir. We were intimate.

Richard Hanley (as noted in chapter 2) wrote a work treating the Star Trek franchise through the lens of analytic philosophy.[5] Much of Hanley's treatment of Start Trek focuses on determining whether or not Data is a person. The fictional character of Data is a challenge to analytic philosophers because his character clearly implies that a machine (Data) is more than the sum of its parts—a machine composed of otherwise inanimate materials has attained an ineffable consciousness. *Next Generation* conveys a number of instances where otherwise inanimate objects possess consciousness.[6]

Life itself, broadly speaking, is a challenge to the analytic philosophy materialist position. As noted in the introduction, the "little pond of goo" from which all life on Earth emanated is conveyed in the *Next Generation* episode "All Goods Things . . ." (1994). It is from this *pond of goo* that the *absolute* for organic life on Earth was born, as here is where the will (i.e., *spirit*) to live/survive/procreate on this planet was spawned.

Returning to the issue of consciousness, this is something that analytic philosophy cannot account for. Ostensibly, the two most cogent interpretations of human consciousness from a materialist standpoint are functionalism and identity theory. Advocates of identity theory hold that the mind is nothing more than biochemical interactions in the brain—in spite of the fact that the biochemical processes of the brain have been thoroughly analyzed and *consciousness* has yet to be located. Functionalism is a theory whereby humans are cast as vessels (computers) that generate outputs in response to inputs (stimuli)—which, if accurate, would reduce free will to nothing more than to a choice of mental states that determine how we respond to stimuli.

Star Trek appropriates the view that human consciousness is a thing-in-itself (as argued by Decartes and Hegel) that transcends the organ of the brain. Star Trek uses this notion as an artistic device. In "Turnabout Intruder" (1969—original series), for instance, Kirk (against his will) has his consciousness switched with another person. Data has his body taken over by another person's consciousness ("The Schizoid Man" 1989—*Next Generation*). The Vulcan Mind Meld is an artistic device reflecting the notion that the mind is not solely a set of (biochemical) processes nor mental states, but a metaphysical entity.

Analytic philosopher, Stephen P. Schwartz, acknowledges that neither identity theory nor functionalism are convincing theories of the human mind. Nevertheless, Schwartz notes (while speaking as a functionalist) that they (as well as all other analytic philosophers) refuse to accept that the human mind cannot be accounted for by materialist explanations: "We are only at the very beginning of the science of mind. No one, at this point, knows how, when, or if consciousness . . . can be explained functionally or in some other way consistent with scientific principles."[7] A textbook case of dogma.

It is noteworthy that comedy/laughter cannot be accounted for by materialist conceptions of the human mind. It is a materialist conception that ostensibly prompts Star Trek's creators to write Data (initially) without the capability to partake in humor. With his mind completely consisting of wires, circuits and electrical impulses, Data is in the dark when it comes to jocularity and sarcasm (*Next Generation*—"The Outrageous Okona" 1988).[8]

CLONES AS A WARRIOR CASTE

Coherent theories of the human mind seemingly indicate that the mind is more than the brain. Nevertheless, we do have artistic representations of sentient beings cloned for military purposes. This suggests that genes can be weaponized in the form of aggressive, ruthless soldiers. Just as importantly, these soldiers can be programmed to blindly obey a particular authority. While this is ostensibly the premise of the artistic device of cloned soldiers, cloned soldiers (as any soldier) require compelling normative reasons to fight and die in battle.

What would it mean to be genetically designed to obey a state, chain of command, or power structure? On the face of it, this has no meaning. Why do people fight in modern warfare? Why do people agree to serve in militaries (formal and informal) actively engaged in warfare? Why do people risk life and limb in such circumstances—particularly in the modern era, when the technologies of death (fully deployed in war) do inflict high numbers of casualties? Clones like everyone have to have a survival instinct. Thus, these questions would be as pertinent to them as anyone else.

In *The Clone Wars* the argument is made that the clones of the series fight because of the band of brothers phenomenon. In other words, they fight for their comrades in arms. Obviously, nothing stops the clones from collectively walking away from the military, or even conspiring to take over the state. The fact that the clones are fighting to protect a Republic from sinister and authoritarian forces presumably gives enough of a normative reason to fight and die. Thus, in this case the clones of *The Clone Wars* are fighting for justice, or, more specifically, to protect a just order.

What are the clones of Star Wars movies fighting for? It is unstated. This lack of normative motive creates a narrative lacuna in these movies. Significantly, the clones of the first three Star Wars movies (*Star Wars*, *Empire Strikes Back*, and *Return of the Jedi*) serve the Empire and are explicitly cast as dim-witted: with mind tricks working easily on them, and their being militarily defeated by Ewoks—a primitive people, who only had sticks and stones to fight with (and with very limited physical abilities), while the clones were equipped with the most advanced weaponry.

The absence of a normative motive to serve the Empire is precisely why U.S. President Ronald Reagan could label the Soviet Union the "Evil Empire" in the 1980s (*à la* Star Wars). By this time the Soviet Union ostensibly lost its normative élan. Stalinist oligarchy, authoritarianism, and terror had made the Soviet state elite's claim to be the bearer of the October Revolution ring hollow. Thus, in the American mind Soviet citizens' commitment to their political order was more the result of inertia than anything else. Hence, when Reagan called the Soviet Union the Evil Empire, this made inherent sense because the normative reasons underlying both was severely lacking.

The normative motives of the Jemh'dar from the Star Trek franchise are more specified. The Jemh'dar are the warrior caste of the Dominion. The Dominion are led by what are called the Founders—a shape-shifting species whose natural state is liquid. Through their leadership of the Jemh'dar (who are industrially breed), the Founders have made the Dominion an imperial power. The reason that the Founders seek out empire is for defensive purposes. This leads us to the ideation of Carl Schmitt.

Carl Schmitt (1888–1985) is in the pantheon of neoconservative thinkers.[9] Schmitt was an architect of the Nazi Germany legal regime and known as the "Crown Jurist" of the Nazis.[10] He held that at the center of politics is the distinction "between friend and enemy."[11] Social and political cohesion is based on this foe/friend dichotomy. Reflective of Schmitt's "friend/enemy" reasoning, in *The Next Generation* episode "Face of the Enemy" (1993) the point is made that Romulans have an "absolute certainty about . . . who is a friend and who is an enemy." Political scientist Shadia B. Drury renders the following observation: "Schmitt . . . believes that politics is first and foremost about the distinction between WE and THEY. [He] thinks that a political order can be stable only if it is united by an external threat."[12] The Star Trek movie *First Contact* (1996)—as noted in chapter 4—is predicated on a WE/THEY distinction.

While Schmitt emphasizes how the friend/foe bifurcation serves to create unity/political cohesion among identity groups, in fact this ideation is a recipe for perpetual violent conflict. By seeking out (perhaps emphasizing) the "difference" of THEY to WE (and worst still, conceptualizing THEY as a potential "foe"), Schmitt's ideation can create paranoia—as every THEY is a potential conqueror. Therefore, conquest/destruction could be cast as self-defense—a preemptive strategy to prevent THEY ("a potential foe") from conquering/destroying/attacking WE. The leadership caste of the Dominion (who are liquid creatures) explains its imperial ambitions in terms of preemptive conquest/empire: "The Solids [humanoids] have always been a threat to us. That's the only the justification we need." "*Because what you control can't hurt you*" (*Deep Space Nine*—"The Search" 1994). In justifying the 2003 invasion of Iraq, the Bush administration claimed that this country possessed weapons of mass destruction that could be used to attack the United States—*not that there was any plan to do so*. Political scientist Anne Norton notes how such reasoning could be used as a basis for perpetual war: "If a nation could attack because it feared not that it might be attacked tomorrow or the next day, or the next month, but in some vague future, who would be immune?"[13] In fact of matter, the Bush administration did more that use the concept of "vague future" threat to attack another country, it employed the THEY idea (the potential foe being Iraq under Saddam Hussein) to conquer this country. Therefore, George W. Bush Administration invoked the idea of *preemptive empire*. Put differently, THEY were conquered before THEY destroyed/conquered WE, and *THEY must be occupied lest they attack WE in the future*—or as the Dominion leader put it, "Because what you control can't hurt you."

While the Founders are motivated by preemptive empire, why do the Jemh'dar fight for the Dominion? The reasons are predominately religious.

The Jemh'dar view the Founders as gods. While the suggestion is made that the Jemh'dar are genetically induced to worship the Founders, is there actually a way to genetically engender adherence to a specific theology? Seemingly not. Maybe genes can be manipulated to make someone more prone to believe in religion, but it is ostensibly impossible to genetically prompt belief in a specified set of religious ideas. (Indicative of this, the Jemh'dar are depicted on occasion as disobeying orders and the chain of command [e.g., *Deep Space Nine*—"To the Death" 1996].) Much more plausible is that the Jemh'dar are indoctrinated (like any other subjugated group) to be subservient to the dominate group—including the state they control. Thus, the Dominion and its political ideology (of the Founders as deities) are a critique of religion—as a potentially authoritarian tool to induce blind obedience and warlike behavior. Conversely, isn't the regimentation of the military a kind of authoritarian religion, intended to induce warlike behavior. Soldiers are indoctrinated (hectored) to obediently submit to the chain of command, and kill when ordered to do so.

Star Trek in other instances has cast theocracy (i.e., political religion) as dangerous and stunting human intellectual development. Hence, political religion is something to be avoided. "All Our Yesterdays" (1969—original series) is an episode where Captain Kirk is transported back to the Puritan period, and comes close to being burned alive for being a "witch." When the Enterprise (in *Next Generation*) is involved in rekindling religious beliefs among a group of primitive people, the point is made "that religion could degenerate into inquisitions, holy wars, chaos" ("Who Watches the Watchers" 1989).

Perhaps the strongest critique of theocracy in the history of American television is posited in "The Apple" (1967—original series). Significantly, the "people of Vaal" are quite dimwitted, as they are completely dependent on Vaal and unable to take care of themselves. Kirk makes the following observation of the natives: "These people aren't living, they're existing. They don't create, they don't produce, they don't even think. They exist to service a machine [i.e., a god]."

CONCLUSION

Derek R. Sweet utilizes *The Clone Wars* to argue that clones are ontologically no different from other human beings. While an artistically credible portrayal of clones seemingly dictates that clones are as autonomous as anyone else, the literary device of human clones raise specific philosophical issues, such as the relationship of sentience to normative values and the metaphysical properties of the human mind.

The Star Trek franchise provides key insight into these issues. Star Trek suggests that sentient beings are connected to the Hegelian Absolute. Taking this argument one step further, the mind is a dialectic process involving the Absolute and the brain. Therefore, Geordi LaForge (who sees with the aid of a prosthetic device) and Lt. Cmdr. Data (an android) view the same normative world. Hence, sentient, intelligent clones would have the same normative autonomy as anyone else.

The creators of the Star Wars franchise do not ascribe any specific normative values to clones, and this creates a narrative flaw (particularly in the first three Star Wars movies). In the case of the Jemh'dar (who comprise the Dominion warrior caste) the Star Trek creators give them a normative motivation in the form of religious beliefs—that is, they worship the leadership caste of the Dominion (the Founders). This can be interpreted as part of the broader critique of political religion manifest in the Star Trek franchise—that is, theocracy as authoritarian.

NOTES

1. Derek R. Sweet, *Star Wars in the Public Sqaure: The Clone Wars as Political Dialogue* (Jefferson, NC: MacFarland, 2015).

2. Stephen E. Levick, *Clone Being: Exploring the Psychological and Social Dimensions* (Lanham, MD: Rowman & Littlefield, 2003); Arlene Judith Klotzko, *A Clone of Your Own?* (New York: Cambridge University Press, 2006).

3. Donald Phillip Verene, *Hegel's Absolute: An Introduction to Reading the Phenomenology of Spirit* (Albany: State University New York Press, 2007); Stephen Houlgate, *Hegel's "Phenomenology of Spirit": A Reader's Guide* (New York: Bloomsbury Academic, 2013); James Kreines, *Reason in the World: Hegel's Metaphysics and its Philosophical Appeal* (New YOrk: Oxford University Press, 2015).

4. (*Next Generation*—"Encounter at Farpoint" 1987).

5. Richard Hanley, *The Metaphysics of Star Trek* (New York: Basic, 1997).

6. (*Next Generation* episodes—"Home Soil" 1988; "Elementary, Dear Data" 1988; "Evolution" 1989; "The Quality of Life" 1992).

7. Stephen P. Schwartz, *A Brief History of Analytic Philosophy: From Russell to Rawls* (West Sussex, UK: Wiley-Blackwell, 2012), 192.

8. Perhaps because a materialist conception of the mind is unrealistic, artistically uninteresting, or both, later, we learn that Data's android "brother," Lore, does have emotions (*Next Generation*—"Datalore" 1988), and Data ultimately comes to have emotions through an "emotion chip" (*Next Generation*—"Brothers" 1990; *Star Trek: Generations* 1994).

9. Anne Norton, *Leo Strauss and the Politics of American Empire* (New Haven, CT: Yale University Press, 2004).

10. Joseph W. Bendersky, *Carl Schmitt: Theorist for the Reich* (Princeton: Princeton University Press, 1983).

11. "The specific political distinction to which political actions and motives can be reduced is that between friend and enemy." Carl Schmitt, *The Concept of the Political*, expanded edition (Chicago: University of Chicago University, 2007 [1929]), 26.

12. Shadia B. Drury, *Leo Strauss and the American Right* (New York: St. Martin's Press, 1997), 23.

13. Norton, *Leo Strauss and the Politics of American Empire*, 143.

Chapter Seven

Art as Knowledge

Who Leads the American World System

Drawing on the philosophy of Georg Hegel[1] (perhaps the most important of continental philosophers), James Kreines holds that *reason in the world* metaphysically exists.[2] *Reasons of the world* are reasons of the Hegelian Absolute. Thus, similar to the fact that gravity is curves in the space-time continuum along which matter moves[3]—reasons are the grooves in the Absolute along which human decision making occurs. Art allows us to conceptualize, understand, speculate about the grooves (reasons) of the Absolute.[4]

One key point from Kreines's position is that the role of social science is to cogitate, explore, identify the reasons of the world that shape social, political norms. Art (particularly popular culture) becomes an important source in identifying the way that people reason about the world and how they perceive political elites reasoning in the world.

Popular culture is germane to understanding contemporary politics because television/movie creators frequently try to attract viewers by conveying *authentic* political motifs. Conversely, viewers seek out *authentic* movies and television shows. This is in contrast to opinion surveys (for instance), as the formation of the data begins with the surveyor seeking to directly solicit an opinion—however impromptu or shallow.

American television over the last twenty-five years has been conveying the decline of U.S. democracy and the rise of authoritarianism. This is particularly evident in the Star Trek franchise, *Justice League Unlimited* (2001–2006), *The Blacklist* (2013–present), and the Netflix series *House of Cards* (2013–2018). Star Trek in the 1990s pointed to political efforts to create a more authoritarian state in the name of national security. In *Justice League Unlimited* political decision making takes place entirely outside of the democratic process. *The Blacklist* indicates that the American government has been taken over by ruthless elements. *House of Cards* depicts what can be labeled palatial, imperial politics.

Authoritarianism

The last episode of season 2 of *Star Trek: Enterprise* ("The Expanse" [2003]) has a terrorist attack committed against Earth—the Florida peninsula. The "probe"—that upon explosion killed 7 million people—was launched from a remote and uncharted area of space known as the Delphic Expanse. The Enterprise crew learns that this probe was only a "test" and a larger explosive is being planned to destroy the entirety of Earth. This attack is being carried out by the "Xindi." Season 3 is dedicated to Enterprises's effort to stop this threat against humanity.

In the aftermath of the 2001 9/11 attack, the Bush administration argued for greater political authority to be vested in the White House—including the power to make war. Using the theory of the Unitary Executive, the Bush White House held that the U.S. Constitution empowered the president to act unilaterally—without consultation or authorization from the legislative or judicial branches of government.[5] Carl Schmitt argued that the executive (the president) under the Weimar constitution had broad discretion to declare a state of emergency—even if only a governing majority could not be established in the Reichstag (parliament). When an effort was made to limit the power of the executive during a "crisis," Schmitt argued against enumerating the executive's powers during such a crisis—thereby standing for open-ended, unfettered executive authority in such circumstances.[6]

In the *Star Trek: Deep Space Nine* episode "Homefront" (1996), a terrorist bombing occurs on Earth—killing twenty-seven. In the aftermath of this attack, Starfleet (i.e., the military) argues for greater security measures. The president of Earth resists this suggestion: "I understand the need for increased security, but . . . ."

> President: I believe the changeling threat is somewhat less serious than Starfleet does.
>
> Admiral Leyton: Mister President, I assure you the threat is real.
>
> President: For all we know, there was only one changeling on Earth, and he may not even be here anymore.
>
> Captain Sisko: But if he is here, we have a problem. There's no telling how much damage one changeling could do.

Art as Knowledge 69

President: Forgive me for saying so, Captain, but you sound a little . . . paranoid

Sisko: Do I?

This exchange presages the Bush administration contention that the Al-Qaeda threat required greater political/legal latitude for the military-security apparatus. President Bush took this position even though the 9/11 attack involved only a handful of perpetrators, many of whom died in the attack.

In the end, the Earth President agrees to the enhanced security measures being proposed by the military. Interestingly, the enhanced security measures are seemingly instituted with simply the president's signature—there are no other deliberations presented or discussed.

These increased security measures are cast as necessary defensive measures to protect "paradise" or utopia (i.e., Earth):

President: I would hate to be remembered as the Federation President who destroyed paradise.

Captain Sisko: We're not looking to destroy paradise, Mister President. We're looking to save it.

Just like the Bush administration argued for enhanced security measures and greater power for the presidency to protect "our American way of life."[7]

In the denouement of "Homefront" Earth experiences a planetary-wide blackout. A state of emergency has been declared. The subsequent *Deep Space Nine* episode "Paradise Lost" (1996) begins by showing platoons of troops patrolling the street, and everyone submitting to security screening (blood tests)—to establish that they are not enemies. We learn that the power outage was perpetrated by elements within the military. Thus, *Deep Space Nine* issues a caution against the use of national security threats to suspend civil and political rights, as well as democratic decision-making processes: "What you're trying to do is seize control of Earth and place it under military rule." "If that's what it takes to stop the Dominion."

Torture as a National Security Device

The Bush administration in 2001 declares the "War on Terror," and as part of this war orders the invasion of Afghanistan—where Al-Qaeda is headquartered. As the United States is taking prisoners in Afghanistan, the Bush administration designates many of them to be "enemy combatants"—therefore denying them Geneva Convention protections, including the prohibition against torturing prisoners of war.[8] The United States opens the Guantanamo prison camp in 2002 to house these so-called enemy combatants—where "aggressive interrogation" (i.e., torture techniques) against these prisoners were authorized.[9] The movie *Zero Dark Thirty* (2012) (made in close collaboration with the U.S. military and the Central Intelligence Agency) indicates that torture is used by the U.S. government in its dealings abroad.[10] Additionally, in 2013 the *New York Times* reported that "[a] nonpartisan, independent review of interrogation and detention programs in the years after the September 11, 2001, terrorist attacks concludes that 'it is indisputable that the United States engaged in the practice of torture' and that the nation's highest officials bore ultimate responsibility for it."[11]

The episode *Star Trek: Enterprise* "Anomaly" aired September 2003 and offers a storyline whereby torture is needed to protect Earth from attack. This paralleled Bush administration arguments at the time that "enhanced interrogation" techniques were required to protect the United States from further attack.[12] Shortly after entering the Delphic Expanse to stop the planned destruction of Earth, the Enterprise's fuel stock is pirated: "They took every one of our antimatter storage pods." Without these pods, Enterprise will run out of fuel in a month—"tops." In the raid against Enterprise one of the pirates is captured. Information from this captive (Orgoth) is the only way that Enterprise can retrieve its much needed fuel. Archer tries to intimidate Orgoth into cooperating, but Orgoth holds that "I don't think you'd be very comfortable torturing another man. You and your crewmates are far too civilized for that. Too moral." Captain Archer tells him otherwise: "I need what was stolen from me. There's too much at stake to let my morality get in the way." Orgoth: "Are you taking me to your torture chamber?" Archer puts Orgoth in an "airlock"—which Archer uses to suffocate Orgoth. Orgoth relents and tells the Captain what he wants to know. Enterprise recovers her much needed fuel. The use of suffocation as a torture technique by *Enterprise* is significant in that the most prominent torture technique deployed by the Bush administration was "waterboarding"—whereby victims feel as if they are suffocating through simulated drowning.[13]

In the 2005 *Justice League Unlimited* episode "Question Authority" a secret U.S. intelligence agency (Cadmus—see below) tortures The Question. (The Question's only super ability is a critical/forensic mind.) The Question's unnamed torturer demands that he divulge what he learned from viewing classified computer files—somewhat presaging the WikiLeaks controversy.[14] The Question refuses to relent. As The Question is screaming in agony, the torturer tells him the electric shock torture "will continue until I break you." Sadistically, he adds, "Perhaps even afterward." Kevin D. Williams, in comparing *Justice League* in the 2000s with an earlier iteration of the Justice League show aired in the 1970s (titled *Superfriends*), explains that the show in the 2000s more starkly conveys violence:

> If the use of superpowers is a metaphor for the use of American power, Superfriends and Justice League represent starkly contrasting political philosophies. . . . There is an odd paradox between the series, in that *Justice League* superheroes are shown taking much more punishment than *Superfriends*; however, *Justice League* superheroes are capable of being bruised and cut (we never see a cut or bruise in *Superfriends*).

This is seemingly the result of the fact that the U.S. foreign policy establishment is more violent today than in the 1970s: "These representations mirror the conducting of military actions during their respective times. . . . Both series clearly reflect these differences in action and conflict. *Superfriends* downplays and sanitizes its violence, whereas *Justice League* portrays it as punishing and brutal."[15]

Democracy in Retreat

The *Justice League Unlimited* animated television series conveys the inherent lack of democracy in the operation of the current world system. *Justice League* (2001–2004) draws on the DC Comics stable of superhero characters: Superman, Wonder Woman, The Flash, Martian Manhunter (a.k.a. J'onn J'onzz, pronounced Jon Jones), Batman, Hawk Girl, and the Green Lantern. The show is later retitled *Justice League Unlimited* (2004–2006) and groups together innumerable superheroes. The superhero genre *in toto* seemingly suggests that democracy within the context of present-day modernity is an impossibility. Reynolds observes that the superhero is "beyond the power of the armed forces, should he choose to oppose state power."[16] In the context of capitalism, the powers of modernity are directed by capitalists—who pursue wealth, power, ego gratification, and so on. Significantly, there is no election, or democratic process, to determine who will gain super powers, and, similarly, there is no mechanism that would allow the public to take away such powers. The result is some with super powers are "good" (thereby deemed super heroes) and some are "bad" (i.e., super villains). The public, in the final instance, simply has to hope that the superheroes out maneuver the super villains.[17]

In *Justice League Unlimited* we see the league overtly taking on the role of a government—identifying risks/crises throughout the world (even the galaxy) and deploying the appropriate response (i.e., superheroes). One scene conveys the league overseeing/conducting "23 active missions" ("To Another Shore" 2005). The Justice League, for instance, evacuates people threatened by an erupting volcano on a Carribean island—"San Mateo" ("The Doomsday Sanction" 2005).

In episode "The Ties That Bind" (2005), we see the Justice League making foreign policy decisions. Factions on another planet are engaging in intrigue. The Martian Manhunter (representing the political will of the league) decides not to intervene, arguing that the league's intervention could result in "[a] dictator who could eventually threaten Earth." He adds "better to let them fight amongst themselves." Flash decides on his own to intervene. There is no democratic decision-making process (or appeal to elected officials) to decide these foreign policy matters. The episode "A Better World" (2003) involves an alternate reality, where we see the league take total state power, and in so doing establishes an authoritarian/draconian global regime.

Therefore, in *Justice League Unlimited* we see a world system whereby the public is outside of the framework of political decision making. In the real world, the U.S. foreign policy apparatus is the most insulated aspect of government—with the national security state operating under a veil of secrecy (and misinformation [e.g., Iraq's WMDs]).[18]

American elections are no guarantee against tyranny. In *Justice League Unlimited* we see Lex Luther—corporate head and Superman's villainous nemesis—become the leading candidate for the U.S. presidency. (To Luther: "Have you seen the latest polls? You're going to be our next President" ["Question Authority"].) In the "A Better World" alternative reality, Luther becomes president of the United States. Similarly, in *The Blacklist*, Russian billionaire, the nefarious Alexander Kirk, is single-handedly financing the presidential campaign of the lead candidate ("Alexander Kirk" 2016).

The State-within-the-State Phenomenon

Arguably the most significant entry in the history of American television that dons a stance highly critical of the U.S. state is *The Blacklist*. Pointing to the White House, central character Raymond "Red" Reddington matter of factly states in the fourth episode of the series, "People think it matters who occupies that house. It doesn't. Multinational corporations and criminals run the world" ("Gina Zanetakos" 2013). The focus of *The Blacklist* is the multinational corporations and criminals that presumably run the world; Red being one of them.

The most politically substantial aspect of *The Blacklist* is the mysterious network of economic elites and criminal elements that form the "Cabal." It has penetrated the national security state at the highest levels. The "Director of Clandestine Services" and the National Security Advisor both are part of the *Cabal*.

Star Trek: Deep Space Nine in the 1990s did point to the national security apparatus being autonomous and lawless. It did so through the literary device of *Section 31*. *Justice League Unlimited* conveyed the "state within the state" phenomenon in the 2000s with *Cadmus*. The Donald Trump White House points to what amounts to the "state within the state," or what is more popularly known as the "Deep State," to account for domestic machinations against his government.[19]

Section 31

Deep Space Nine introduces "Section 31"—a secret intelligence agency that is outside the law. It is described in the following terms: "We don't submit reports or ask for approval for specific operations, if that's what you mean. We're an autonomous department." In another instance, Section 31 is cast as "judge, jury, and executioner." Section 31 justifies its existence and means in terms consonant with national security: "We deal with threats to the Federation that jeopardize its very survival." "If you knew how many lives we've saved, I think you'd agree that the ends do justify the means."[20]

Section 31 operatives have no scruples. Prior to the advent of open hostilities between the Dominion and the Federation, it infects the changeling Odo (chief of security for the *Deep Space Nine* station) with a deadly disease in the hopes that he will infect his species.[21] Section 31 kidnaps a Starfleet officer (Julian Bashir—chief medical officer of Deep Space Nine); tortures him (through sleep deprivation); and psychologically disorients him into believing he is a Dominion spy. When Bashir states in disbelief, "Is it possible that the Federation would condone this kind of activity?" A Deep Space Nine crew member cynically responds: "I find it hard to believe that they wouldn't. Every other great power has a unit like Section Thirty-One"[22]—an all-powerful, lawless secret security organization. The 2013 Star Trek movie, *Into Darkness*, has Section 31 conduct a false-flag operation to initiate war with the Klingons.

We learn that the Cardassians also operate a secret, autonomous intelligence service—the *Obsidian Order*. "In theory" the Obsidian Order "answer[s] to the political authority . . . , just as the military does. In practice we both run our own affairs" (*Deep Space Nine*—"Defiant" 1994). Later, it is discovered that the Cardassian Obsidan Order and the Romulan *Tal Shiar* (another intelligence agency) secretly constructed a fleet of military ships, and unilaterally undertake an attack on the Dominion home world. ("If you attack the Dominion. . . . [y]ou'll be taking Romulus and Cardassia into war") (*Deep Space Nine*—"Improbable Cause" 1995).

Cadmus

"Cadmus"—a secret U.S. government agency developing/deploying secret weaponry—is formed to counter the Justice League. Cadmus is involved in "secret weapons; illegal cloning experiments; bypassing Congress" ("The Doomsday Sanction"). It is referred to as "a shadow cabinet" and "a black ops group"—with "legitimate connections to the government" ("Flashpoint" 2005). Cadmus, in another instance, is described as a collection of "power brokers, politicians, criminals, and black ops mercenaries" ("Question Authority")—as the Blackwater security outfit, which works closely with the U.S. military and intelligence agencies, might be described.[23] Cadmus is headed by Amanda Waller, who "served in intelligence under three Administrations" ("The Doomsday Sanction"). The U.S. president unilaterally authorizes a Cadmus assault on the league's Watchtower ("Question Authority").

The Blacklist also invokes a Blackwater like organization: Halcyon. It is described as "a private military-intelligence agency who specializes in operations too sophisticated or politically incorrect for anyone else, like working with Israel to sabotage Iran's nuclear program or negotiating with terrorists for the release of hostages . . . in direct violation of American foreign policy." Halcyon is described as above the law: "The White House Counsel specifically told" the FBI "not to investigate Halcyon." The National Security Advisor said the following of Halcyon: "They're powerful, arrogant, and unchecked, but our government depends on them" ("Susan Hargrave" 2016).

The Cabal

Where *The Blacklist* somewhat breaks new ground with its literary device of the Cabal is that the "state within the state" is used by private, corrupt elements to control politics and serve their interests. Thus, with Section 31 and Cadmus the insulated national security apparatus (outside of democratic oversight) is cast as a necessary evil to protect the Federation from its enemies (*Deep Space Nine*) or national governments from the Justice League. The Cabal in controlling the U.S. national security state is motivated entirely by its own agenda. The Cabal wants to reconstitute a bipolar world. (The Cabal "believes there are too many players on the board. [It] thinks a bipolar world is inherently more stable." ["Quon Zhang" 2015]). Thus, the Cabal is the prime architect of American foreign policy and the entire world system.

A similar nefarious network penetrating a state is invoked in *Star Trek: Enterprise*. In 2002 as the neoconservative[24] agenda (i.e., invading Iraq) is gaining momentum, both through the Bush government and the national media—most prominently the *New York Times*[25]—the *Enterprise* episode "Fallen Hero" aired. The Enterprise picks up the Vulcan ambassador to the planet of Mazar—she has been recalled by her government. Soon after Enterprise departs, the Mazar government demands that the Vulcan ambassador (V'lar) return—sending ships in pursuit. After initially refusing to tell Captain Archer the cause of the current controversy, V'lar relents and informs the Captain why the Mazarites are so eager for her return.

> The Mazarites pursuing us are criminals. They are members of an organization that's infiltrated all levels of government, making themselves wealthy and powerful at the expense of many innocent victims. Their methods include eliminating anyone who stands in their way.

She adds that "the corruption ran deeper than I thought."

Palatial/Imperial Politics

House of Cards stands out in its treatment of American politics as palatial politics. Francis Underwood carries out a series of character assassinations in order to become U.S. president. He begins with the vice president, and after he becomes vice president Underwood dispenses with the president—thereby becoming president himself. The successful use of assassination in a polity is indicative of authoritarianism. Authoritarian polities (*empires*) seek to concentrate political and institutional authority in a small number of people—who exercise institutional control and work together to impose their politics and policies on the whole of society.

In turn, this is precisely why the phenomenon of *palatial politics* occurs—people maneuver among the coterie of power wielders to hold and/or attain power. In the *Deep Space Nine* episode "When it Rains . . ." (1999) the argument is made that the Klingon Empire's current head of government (Chancellor Gowron) has no significant accomplishments other than successfully mastering Klingon "palace intrigue":[26] "what has he done except plot and scheme his way to power."

In a context where political power is highly concentrated assassination becomes an effective means of advancing a military/political career (agenda)—as rivals/obstacles are vanquished. Allegations that Russian president Vladimir Putin aided in the installation of Donald J. Trump as U.S. president[27] can be interpreted as an effort to politically destroy Trump (i.e., character assassination) and replace his regime with one that is more hostile to Russia.[28] In the Empire universe of "Mirror, Mirror" (1967—*Star Trek*, the original series), "Captain Kirk's enemies have a habit of disappearing" (via a technology of assassination—the "Tantalus field"). The Klingon Empire's chancellor, K'mpec, is poisoned to open the path to power for an ambitious clan (*Next Generation*—"Reunion" 1990). In the *Deep Space Nine* episode "Inter Arma Enim Silent Leges" (1999), a clandestine operation is successfully executed to manipulate the politics of the Romulan Star Empire by politically destroying a "Senator" to ensure the appointment of a reliable Federation ally to the Romulan "Continuing Committee"—the highest policymaking body in the Empire. Assassination resulting in the protection/entrenchment of a policy regime brings to mind the President John F. Kennedy assassination, as his killing seemingly cleared the way for a more reliable "Cold War Warrior" in Lyndon B. Johnson to ascend to the American presidency.[29] Currently, there is seemingly an effort to assassinate the character of President Donald Trump as an agent of the Russian Putin government.[30]

Season five of *House of Cards* (2017) is especially noteworthy—as it focuses on Underwood's effort to cling to power in the context of an election and its aftermath. The normative core of this season is *political stability*—as this is the normative core of empire. In other words, why authoritarian regimes and empires persist is because they promise political (economic, social) stability. The invocation of terrorism is actually a way to terrorize the public into supporting an authoritarian regime (including its military adventurism), as such adventurism and authoritarianism are held to be necessary in order to maintain stability (i.e., a well-functioning society). Leading up to the presidential election, Underwood "wags the dog" to a virtually absurd level—making terrorism the entirety of his campaign and he successfully uses the specter of "computer" terrorism to upend the election (as he was about to lose).

What is particularly significant is the skullduggery of Underwood and his wife (Claire—now vice president) to cover-up his illegal (election) machinations, as well as the murders he committed on his rise to power. The Underwoods engineer or directly commit murder in order to hide their secrets. Again, this bespeaks a politics of stability—as the coming to light of these immoral, murderous deeds would bring down the Underwoods' government and damage the (credibility) of the American state. The U.S. government classifies an immense amount of information in an effort to protect the image of the American state.[31]

CONCLUSION

Drawing on the Hegelian concept of the Absolute, my argument is that social scientists should focus their scholarly attention on the reasons of the Absolute—or as James Kreines put it, *reason in the world*. People operate through *reason in the world*—as do political elites. Art (good art[32]) allows us to cogitate reason in the world, and particularly the reasoning underlying the actions of political elites. Popular art is of particular significance as creators and broad audiences will "connect" through *authentic art*—that is, art that seemingly conveys reason in the world.

In this chapter, I have identified the Star Trek franchise and three television series that convey the reasoning of political elites. All three are critical of the reasoning of contemporary U.S. political elites. Star Trek, beginning in the 1990s, indicated that there are conspiracies afoot to establish authoritarian government under the guise of national security. *Justice League Unlimited* in the 2000s presented a foreign policy-making process that is beyond democratic oversight—including the use of torture. The *Star Trek* original series ("Cloud Minders" 1969—as described in chapter 4) and *Justice League Unlimited* point to the use of torture to punish perceived political enemies, whereas *Star Trek: Enterprise* adopts the contemporary U.S. government view that torture is needed to forward national security. *Star Trek: Deep Space Nine* and *Justice League Unlimited* both portray intelligence agencies as dangerously outside of the law. The American television series *The Blacklist* is particularly noteworthy because it indicates that a private set of elites is profoundly shaping U.S. foreign policy and the world system itself to serve their own ends. Finally, *House of Cards* draws on the palatial politics that arguably shapes Washington D.C. politics.

NOTES

1. Donald Phillip Verene, *Hegel's Absolute: An Introduction to Reading the Phenomenology of Spirit* (Albany: State University New York Press, 2007); Stephen Houlgate, *Hegel's "Phenomenology of Spirit": A Reader's Guide* (New York: Bloomsbury Academic, 2013); Brady Bowman, *Hegel and the Metaphysics of Absolute Negativity* (Cambridge: Cambridge University Press, 2015); Andrew Feenberg, *Technosystem: The Social Life of Reason* (Cambridge, MA: Harvard University Press, 2017).

2. James Kreines, *Reason in the World: Hegel's Metaphysics and Its Philosophical Appeal* (New York: Oxford University Press, 2015).

3. A. Zee, *Einstein Gravity in a Nutshell* (Princeton: Princeton University Press, 2013).

4. William Maker, ed., *Hegel and Aesthetics* (Albany: State University of New York Press, 2000); Kirk Pillow, *Sublime Understanding: Aesthetic Reflection in Kant and Hegel* (Cambridge, MA: MIT Press, 2000); Paul Gordon, *Art as the Absolute: Art's Relation to Metaphysics in Kant, Fichte, Schelling, Hegel, and Schopenhauer* (New York: Bloomsbury Academic, 2015).

5. Jonathan Mahler, "After the Imperial Presidency," *New York Times Magazine*, November 9, 2008, MM42; Ryan J. Barilleaux and Christopher S. Kelley, eds., *The Unitary Executive and the Modern Presidency* (College Station: Texas A&M University Press, 2010).

6. Joseph W. Bendersky, *Carl Schmitt: Theorist for the Reich* (Princeton: Princeton University Press, 1983), chap. 4.

7. "After the Attacks: Bush's Remarks to Cabinet and Advisers," *New York Times*, September 13, 2001. Web; Barilleaux and Kelley, *The Unitary Executive and the Modern Presidency*.

8. "Rewriting the Geneva Conventions," *New York Times*, August 14, 2006, A20.

9. Richard W. Stevenson, "White House says Prisoner Policy Set Humane Tone," *New York Times*, June 23, 2004, A1.

10. Scott Shane, "Portrayal of C.I.A. Torture in Bin Laden Film Reopens a Debate," *New York Times*, December 13, 2012, A1; "About Those Black Sites," *New York Times*, February 18, 2013, A16.

11. Scott Shane, "U.S. Practice Torture after 9/11, Nonpartisan Review Concludes," *New York Times*, April 16, 2013, A1; also see Mark Mazzetti, "Panel Faults C.I.A. over Brutality toward Terrorism Suspects," *New York Times*, December 10, 2014, A1; "Dark again after the Torture Report," *New York Times*, December 12, 2014, A34.

12. "Effort to Prohibit Waterboarding Fails in House," Associated Press, March 12, 2008. Web.

13. Scott Shane, "Waterboarding Used 266 Times on 2 Suspect," *New York Times*, April 20, 2009, A1.

14. Scott Shane and Andrew W. Lehren, "Leaked Cables Offer Raw Look at U.S. Diplomacy," *New York Times*, November 29, 2010, A1; Geoffroy de Lagasnerie, *The Art of Revolt: Snowden, Assange, Manning* (Stanford: Stanford University Press, 2017).

15. Kevin D. Williams, "(R)Evolution of the Television Superhero: Comparing *Superfriends* and *Justice League* in Terms of Foreign Relations," *Journal of Popular Culture*, 44, no. 6 (2011), 1338–1339.

16. Richard Reynolds, *Super Heroes: A Modern Mythology* (Jackson: University Press of Mississippi, 1992), 15.

17. Terry Kading, "Drawn into 9/11, But Where Have All the Superheroes Gone?," in Jeff McLaughlin, ed. *Comic as Philosophy* (Jackson: University Press of Mississippi, 2005);

George A. Gonzalez, "*Justice League Unlimited* and the Politics of Globalization," *Foundation: The International Review of Science Fiction* 45, no. 123 (2016): 5–13.

18. Terry H. Anderson, *Bush's Wars* (New York: Oxford University Press, 2011); Roger Z. George and Harvey Rishikoff, *The National Security Enterprise: Navigating the Labyrinth* (Washington, D.C.: Georgetown University Press, 2011); Michael P. Colaresi, *Democracy Declassified: The Secrecy Dilemma in National Security* (New York: Oxford University Press, 2014).

19. Julie Hirschfeld Davis, "'Deep State'? Until Now, It Was a Foreign Concept," *New York Times*, March 7, 2017, A19.

20. (*Deep Space Nine*—"Inquisition" 1998).

21. (*Deep Space Nine*—"Extreme Measures" 1999).

22. (*Deep Space Nine*—"Inquisition" 1998).

23. Shane and Lehren, "Leaked Cables Offer Raw Look at U.S. Diplomacy"; James Risen, "Before Shooting in Iraq, Warning on Blackwater," *New York Times*, June 30, 2014, A1; James Risen and Mark Mazetti, "Case Ends Against Ex-Blackwater Officials," *New York Times*, February 22, 2013, A16.

24. Gary Dorrien, *The Neoconservative Mind: Politics, Culture, and the War of Ideology* (Philadelphia: Temple University Press, 1993), and *Imperial Designs: Neoconservatism and the New Pax Americana* (New York: Routledge, 2004); John Ehrman, *The Rise of Neoconservatism: Intellectuals and Foreign Affairs, 1945–1994* (New York: Cambridge University Press, 1995); Murray Friedman, *The Neoconservative Revolution: Jewish Intellectuals and the Shaping of Public Policy* (New York: Cambridge University Press, 2005); Benjamin Balint, *Running Commentary: The Contentious Magazine That Transformed the Jewish Left Into the Neoconservative Right* (New York: Public Affairs, 2010); Thomas L. Jeffers, *Norman Podhoretz: A Biography* (New York: Cambridge University Press, 2010); C. Bradley Thompson, with Yaron Brook, *Neoconservatism: An Obituary for an Idea* (Boulder, CO: Paradigm Publishers, 2010); Justin Vaïsse, *Neoconservatism: The Biography of a Movement* (Cambridge, MA: Harvard University Press, 2010); Jean-François Drolet, *American Neoconservatism: The Politics and Culture of a Reactionary Idealism* (New York: Columbia University Press, 2011).

25. Don Van Natta, Jr., Adam Liptak, and Clifford J. Levy, "The Miller Case: A Notebook, A Cause, a Jail Cell and a Deal," *New York Times*, October 16, 2005, sec. 1, p. 1.

26. In the *Star Trek: Voyager* episode "Author, Author" (2001) Klingon politics are referred to as "palace intrigue."

27. Matt Flegenheimer and Scott Shane, "Bipartisan Voices Back U.S. Agencies on Russia Hacking," *New York Times*, Jan. 6, 2017, A1; Nicholas Fandos and Sharon LaFraniere, "Two Reports on Meddling: Choose Your Own Verdict," *New York Times*, April 28, 2018, A14.

28. "Mr. Trump and Mr. Putin, Best Frenemies," *New York Times*, June 29, 2018, A26; Michelle Goldberg, "Trump Shows the World He's Putin's Lackey," *New York Times*, July 17, 2018, A21; Sheryl Gay Stolberg, Nicholas Fandos, and Thomas Kaplan, "Measured Condemnation But No G.O.P. Plan to Act," *New York Times*, July 17, 2018, A1.

29. Robert Dallek *Lyndon B. Johnson: Portrait of a President* (New York: Oxford University Press, 2005); James N. Giglio, *The Presidency of John F. Kennedy* (Lawrence: University of Kansas Press, 2006); Godfrey Hodgson, *JFK and LBJ: The Last Two Great Presidents* (New Haven: Yale University Press, 2015).

30. Scott Shane and Mark Mazzetti, "The Plot to Subvert an Election," *New York Times*, September 20, 2018. Web; Adam Goldman, Michael S. Schmidt, and Nicholas Fandos, "F.B.I. Investigated if Trump Worked for the Russians," *New York Times*, January 12, 2019, A1.

31. Marc Ambinder and D. B. Grady, *Deep State: Inside the Government Secrecy Industry* (Hoboken, NJ: Wiley, 2013). Colaresi, *Democracy Declassified*.

32. Lawrence Levine, *Highbrow/Lowbrow: The Emergence of Cultural Hierarchy in America* (Cambridge, MA: Harvard University Press, 1990); Jason T. Eberl and Kevin S. Decker, eds., *Star Trek and Philosophy: The Wrath of Kant* (Chicago: Open Court, 2008).

Chapter Eight

Popular Culture and Trump Politics

Breaking Bad (2008–2013) works artistically, because it reflects and critiques the political values and norms that predominate under the global neoliberalist regime. My position is these reflections and critiques provide insight into the Trump phenomenon—the installation as U.S. president (in 2017) of someone (Donald J. Trump) who is a hyper-nationalist[1] and highly critical of the neoliberal trade regime.[2] Thus, the argument animating this chapter is that popular culture aids in understanding, analyzing[3]—even predicting/foreshadowing—political, social phenomena (e.g., the rise of Donald Trump).[4]

At the core of *Breaking Bad* are two suppositions—the economic, social gap between the have and have-nots is a dominant feature of American society, and the difference between the have and have-nots is that the former have the "Will the Power."[5] What this means in practice is that those that abide by conventional morality and ethics will remain as have-nots, whereas those that don't can be one of the haves. Even more broadly, *Breaking Bad* indicates that the neoliberalist global system rewards immoral behavior and by implication the wealthy and the corporate elite don't abide by conventional morality.[6]

Drawing on *Breaking Bad*, and other instances of popular culture, allows us to see that "will to power" politics are inherently unstable and globally dangerous. Conversely, *Star Trek: Voyager* episode "The Void" (2001) indicates that collaboration and solidarity are the only means for a stable, thriving world.

The Politics of Neoliberalism

Walter H. White, the protagonist of *Breaking Bad*, is initially presented as a symbol of the ill treatment and poor regard for public service workers in the contemporary period. Walter is a public school chemistry teacher who seemingly garners little respect from his students. The idea that public school teachers are held in low esteem is conveyed via his brother-in-law (Hank): describing Walter's career, life as a "dead-end" ("Caballo sin Nombre" 2010). In another instance, in a party composed of the well-to-do Walter is embarrassed, reticent to acknowledge that he's a high school teacher ("Gray Matter" 2008).

Walter is a skilled chemist (who contributed to a project that was awarded the Nobel Peace Prize) but yet he has virtually nothing to show for it. Additionally (we are told) that as his research partners decided to commercialize their research, Walter opted-out. Walter's research ultimately helped launch a billion dollar company and fortune. His wife, Skyler, is pregnant and cannot work, so Walter is forced to wash cars to make ends meet. The most degrading, demeaning aspect of it all is that when Walter is diagnosed with stage 3 cancer, his health insurance won't cover the best, most successful treatment available. Thus, Walter's seeming credo up until this point of pursuing knowledge/science/chemistry as its own reward and working as a community worker has not only resulted in a life of drudgery, barely above poverty, but will now potentially leave his family with a massive, crushing debt (which he may not be around to help pay off).

Within a context of neoliberalism it can be debated whether everyone is given ample opportunity to fully utilize and maximize their skills, abilities. (P.J., an on-again off-again drug addict, drug dealer, can play the piano beautifully ["Hazard Pay" 2012]). It is evident that Walter is a brilliant talented chemist, and the fact that his talents are effectively sidelined in the formal economy prompts him to apply his capabilities to making ("cooking") the best methamphetamine (aka "crystal meth") on the market.

What is clearer is that, as a result of deindustrialization and automation, many low, no-skilled workers have very limited employment opportunities[7] (we see that Beneke Fabricators [a manufacturing concern operating in New Mexico] is driven out of business by low-cost imports ["Bug" 2011]). This reality is ostensibly pushing untold millions of people toward the drug trade and toward drug use.[8] This is artistically represented in *Breaking Bad* when Jesse Pinkman, who did not finish high school, can only find low-paying menial work—twirling advertising signs all day in the oppressive New Mexico heat and sun. Jesse quits his quest for work in the formal sector and returns to the drug trade and his addiction ("Gray Matter").

The response of the state to the reality that large numbers are seemingly driven to drugs (both as users and providers) by a formal economy that is providing too few adequate jobs is repression. Artistically, symbolically, the militaristic response to the drug trade is represented by the *Breaking Bad* character of Hank Schrader (an agent for the Drug Enforcement Administration [DEA])—who sees the world in black-white (and who regularly derides drug users, dealers as "scum" and the like).

Official thinking toward the poor and dispossessed is conveyed in the *Blue Bloods* (2009–present) episode "School of Hard Knocks" (2018). This series focuses on the New York City police department. The episode in question engages the attitude of public school teachers in poorer, less well-to-do neighborhoods: "Those kids in [the classroom]—I can't save all of them or even most of them. But every year I spot one or two . . . Kids I can help. Kids who want a shot at a decent life." What happens to the rest of the "kids"?—drugs, poverty? A police detective notes, "We can't change this neighborhood," but we can "show . . . that gang violence won't be tolerated." In others words, even among the most humane, thoughtful people within the state, the prime response to social, economic decay and desperation is deterrence (police, prison).

The Politics of Will to Power (or Supermen)

A theoretically significant (unique) aspect of *Breaking Bad* is Walter as a Superman—who is above the moral norms of society. Nietzschean reasoning is conveyed in the following dialogue from the series "Pilot" episode (2008) (when Walter discusses chemistry with his high school students): "It is growth, then decay, then transformation." The insinuation is that morality, ethics, and society are not fixed but shift, change, and are transformed over time. Walter touches on this when he discusses with Hank (a Drug Enforcement Agent [DEA]) that crystal meth was legal and only recently became illegal ("A No-Rough-Stuff-Type Deal" 2008).

What makes Walter a Superman (in addition to his skill as a chemist) is his ability to disregard conventional morality and act immorally. Jesse Pinkman, Walter's partner in crime, does not do well living outside of conventional morality—falling into drug addiction, profound guilt, and deep depression. The ability of Walter to thrive in the cut-throat drug trade is clearly manifest when his crew murders a child to cover up a crime. Jesse is visibly disturbed after the murder, whereas Walter blithely whistles. Walter's ease shakes Jesse ("Dead Freight" 2012). Indicative of how Walter has no ethical, moral qualms with regard to murder, and so on, is when Skyler expresses fear that the dangerous elements within the drug trade will harm him or his family. Walter expresses his innate ruthlessness when he says, "I'm the danger." He adds, "A guy opens his door and gets shot, and you think that of me? No. I am the one who knocks" ("Cornered" 2011).

While Walter is dangerous, is he immoral? Nietzsche held that conventional morality is for the common person, but not for the elite—the Supermen of the world.[9] Within the context of neoliberalism, it is the immoral (according to convention) that succeed. This is patently evident with Walter—who is able to pay for his cancer treatment and achieve financial security for his family only because of a life of crime (including murder). Among the corporate elite, it is those that act ruthlessly (with no regard to community, fairness, and so on) that excel. Are the corporate elite morally any better or worse than Walter? Shifting manufacturing production worldwide in order to maximize profit is the norm in the world today.[10] The fact that this destroys lives and communities is treated as inconsequential.[11]

As to the question of murder, in *Breaking Bad* the owners of the firm Gray Matters accrue a massive fortune by only offering medical treatment to those that can afford to pay for it—presumably allowing others to die. In 2003 the U.S. state illegally invaded Iraq, resulting in the death of untold numbers. The Obama White House directly oversaw the drone assassination program—with the president acting as judge, juror, and executioner.[12] In the denouement of *Breaking Bad*, Walter White dies in the pose of a crucifix. He's being sacrificed to maintain the fiction that society is shaped by morality, as well as to cover up, obscure the immorality of elites ("Felina" 2013).

While Nietzsche may ask us to reserve judgement of Supermen—who may be the dynamic forces of society (moving it toward a new equilibrium)—*Breaking Bad* demonstrates the instability of what can be deemed "radical aristocratic" politics.[13] Walter White and the drug lord Gus Fring (putatively two Supermen) distrust one another and ultimately engage in a cat and mouse game—whereby both actively seek to eliminate the other. When Walter kills Gus, he declares, "I won" ("Face Off" 2011).

The Star Trek franchise is even more explicit and pointed in critiquing Nietzschean thinking with regard to Supermen. In Star Trek historiography, in the Earth's past (or our near future) there is a Eugenics War—"an improved breed of human. That's what the Eugenics War was all about." The war resulted when "young *supermen*" seized "power simultaneously in over forty nations. . . . They were aggressive, arrogant. They began to battle among themselves."[14]

Thus, radical aristocratic politics at the highest (international) realm will almost invariably lead to global tensions and even (nuclear) war as Supermen defy conventional morality and will their nations to power (global hegemony).[15] U.S. president Donald J. Trump explicitly holds that he places America above all else.[16] In a 2017 speech to the United Nations, Trump declared, "I will always put America first"[17]—similarly, the German Nazis would like to emphasize "Germany above all else" (Deutschland über alles).[18]

The most extreme and dangerous/destructive example of the will to power in human history is that of the German Nazi regime.[19] Star Trek warns against Nazism/fascism—indicating that it is predicated on genocidal hate and poses a profound threat to civilization. "Patterns of Force" (1968—original series) portrays a Nazi regime on the planet of Ekos—which was instituted/sponsored/overseen by a Federation official. With Nazism as the political basis of Ekos, the Ekosians organize around the vilification of Zeons—a population from the neighboring planet of Zeon. ("Why do the Nazis hate Zeons?" "Because without us to hate, there'd be nothing to hold them together. So the Party has built us into a threat, a disease to be wiped out.") In addition to massacring the Zeons on Ekos ("the eliminations have started. Within an hour, the Zeon blight will forever be removed from Ekos"), the Nazi regime organizes a planned genocide ("Their Final Solution") against Zeons on their home planet: "Our entire solar system will forever be rid of the disease that was Zeon."

In *Star Trek: Voyager* "The Killing Game" (1998) a German Nazi officer emphasizes the putative greatness of Germany's past to justify its push for worldwide conquest (i.e., their will to power):

> He's never embraced the Führer or his vision. One does not co-operate with decadent forms of life, one hunts them down and eliminates them. The Kommandant speaks of civilization. The ancient Romans were civilised. The Jews are civilised. But in all its moral decay, Rome fell to the spears of our ancestors as the Jews are falling now. Look at our destiny! The field of red, the purity of German blood. The blazing white circle of the sun that sanctified that blood. No one can deny us, no power on Earth or beyond. Not the Christian Savior, not the God of the Jews. We are driven by the very force that gives life to the universe itself!

The kind of hyper-nationalism (will to power) advocated by the likes of the Nazis is extremely dangerous in the modern era—nuclear war, global warming. Therefore, the parable of the Xindi must be taken seriously. As described in chapter 4, the Xindi destroyed their planet as a result of their racialist/nationalist competition.

Much of the intrigue in season one of Amazon Prime series *The Man in the High Castle* (2015–present) revolves around the fact that the Germans have the atomic bomb, while the Japanese do not. (In this series the Germans and the Japanese won World War II and they divided the world among themselves.) This creates ambitions among certain Nazi political elite to engage in a war with Japan. A high-ranking Nazi decides to pass along atomic weaponry science to the Japanese in the hopes of maintaining a balance of power, thereby avoiding another war. The Japanese high command expresses no desire for a balance of power, but seeks nuclear superiority in order to militarily overtake the Nazis—that is, the will to power.

The Rejection of Neoliberalist Politics, Values

The creators of the *Star Trek: Voyager* episode "The Void" make an explicit claim of the importance of operating on foundational principles.[20] Voyager is trapped in a "void" in space (where there is no "matter of any kind"). Other ships trapped in the void have taken up the practice of attacking/raiding other trapped ships for supplies as a means of surviving. ("There are more than one hundred fifty ships within scanning range but I'm only detecting life signs on twenty nine of them.")

A captain from one of the other stranded ships advises Voyager to abandon her ethical principles in the Void: "Wait a few weeks until your resources start to run out. Morality won't keep your life support systems running." Implying she would die for her principles, Captain Janeway responds, "I'm sorry, General. There are some compromises I won't make."

Nonetheless, members of Voyager's crew, in retrieving stolen supplies, suggest that they take supplies from another ship that never belonged to them. Janeway, nevertheless, refuses to act unethically—even while acknowledging other ship captains in the void would not limit themselves by ethical considerations.

> Tuvok: I'm detecting large quantities of food on his supply deck.
>
> Chakotay: Maybe we should take it while we have the chance.
>
> Captain Janeway: Is it ours?
>
> Tuvok: No, but our own reserves are running out.
>
> Chakotay: Valen (the commander of the ship in question) wouldn't hesitate to take it from us.
>
> Captain Janeway: No, he wouldn't. We've got what's ours. Reverse course.

After Captain Janeway refused to take other than what was taken from Voyager, her most senior officers (Tuvok and Chakotay) approach her about this decision.

> Chakotay: We want to be clear about what our policy's going to be while we're here in the Void.
>
> Janeway: You think we should have taken Valen's food.

Tuvok: Logic suggests we may have to be more opportunistic if we intend to survive.

Chakotay: We may not like Valen's tactics but he and his crew are still alive after five years in here.

In response to the conundrum Voyager is seemingly facing in the Void (to be ethical or to survive), Janeway looks for answers in the foundational document of the Federation (the interstellar organization that humans lead): "the Federation Charter."

Chakotay: No section on how to exist in a void.

Janeway: No, but I've become convinced that we've got to stick to our principles, not abandon them.

Chakotay: Should the crew be ready to die for those principles?

Janeway: If the alternative means becoming thieves and killers ourselves, yes.

Thus, Janeway reiterates her willingness to die for her (Federation) principles.

However, in a direct rebuke of "will to power" reasoning, Janeway asserts that principled action leads to the optimal outcome. Specifically, she holds that by behaving in a principled manner Voyager can build social capital among the ships trapped in the Void. Through collaboration and solidarity, Janeway argues the ships in the Void can work together to escape. In shaping this reasoning, Janeway draws inspiration from the example of the Federation: "The Federation is based on mutual co-operation. The idea that the whole is greater than the sum of its parts. Voyager can't survive here alone, but if we form a temporary alliance with other ships maybe we can pool our resources and escape." Voyager shares its limited food and medical supplies, as well as joins in common defense, to build trust and establish (what Janeway calls) the "Alliance." Through the Alliance, Voyager's food supplies are enhanced ("One of the crews that joined us had technology that tripled our replicator efficiency. . . . We can feed five hundred people a day now using half the power it took us a few days ago.") Led by Voyager, the Alliance ships escape the Void. Those that refused to become members stay behind.

Villains That Elide Ethics

Voyager stands out for the fact that a number of its antagonists are villains (or "bad guys") precisely because they elide moral principles (the "will to power"). This sets *Voyager* apart from other science fiction/fantasy genres, where villains are dastardly not because they lack moral principles (per se) but because of their ultimate goals (e.g., attaining ill-gotten gain [e.g., stealing]; inflicting wanton destruction; seeking revenge; capturing political power, and so on).[21] In the case of *Voyager*, the audience can, broadly speaking, sympathize with its antagonists' goals (survival, arriving at a trade deal, and technological advancement), but the villains are "bad guys" precisely because they show little/no scruples is seeking to attain these goals. Three *Voyager* episodes are noteworthy for their villainous pragmatists: "Phage" (1995); "Think Tank" (1999); and "Future's End" (1996).

"Phage"

As a seeming critique of neo-*pragmatism*, the species known as Vidiians is introduced in the episode "Phage." The Vidiians suffer from a condition called the Phage. The Phage destroys the organs of the Vidiians. In response they steal organs from others to survive. ("We are gathering replacement organs and suitable bio-matter. It is the only way we have to fight the phage.") Thus, the Vidiians have established an *intersubjective agreement*[22] that does not respect/recognize the rights of others to their bodies/organs. ("Our society has been ravaged. Thousands die each day. There is no other way for us to survive.") Janeway is dismayed that the Vidiians would accept the practice of organ theft: "I can't begin to understand what your people have gone through. They may have found a way to ignore the moral implications of what you are doing, but I have no such luxury." Janeway will not take back the organs that were stolen from one of her crew because it would result in the death of their current recipient.

"Think Tank"

In "Think Tank" Voyager finds itself being pursued by a species known as the Hazari. It is unable to elude them, and Voyager is in serious danger of being destroyed. As they face this peril, an organization that Janeway dubs the Think Tank ("a small group of minds") appears offering Voyager the knowledge necessary to escape the Hazari. But in exchange for this knowledge, the Think Tank wants (Voyager crew member) Seven of Nine to join their group. We learn that the Think Tank regularly offers knowledge/help in exchange for some prize (normally knowledge).

> We have helped hundreds of clients. We turned the tide in the war between the Bara Plenum and the Motali Empire. Re-ignited the red giants of the Zai Cluster. Just recently, we found a cure for the Vidiian phage. . . . Just last month we helped retrieve a Lyridian child's runaway pet. A subspace meso-

morph, I might add. We had to invent a whole new scanning technology just to find it.

And what did you ask for as compensation?

> One of their transgalactic star charts. The best map of the known galaxy ever created. When we helped the citizens of Rivos Five resist the Borg, all we asked for was the recipe for their famous zoth-nut soup.

Janeway probes the Think Tank's moral/ethical boundaries by asking, "Tell me, is there any job you won't do?" The spokesperson for the group (Kurros—played by Jason Alexander [of "Seinfeld" fame]) explains, "We will not participate in the decimation of an entire species, nor will we design weapons of mass destruction."

Nevertheless, the Think Tank has few scruples in seeking to attain prizes—in this case Seven of Nine. (While human, she is a former member of the Borg collective. Borg modifications have made Seven highly intelligent and capable of telepathic communication.) It was the Think Tank that set the Hazari on Voyager (by placing a bounty on it). In the end, Voyager is able to outmaneuver the Think Tank. But before it is forced to flee, Kurros tells Seven of Nine that she will be dissatisfied living on Voyager, and would have been happier with them—living a life of contemplation and knowledge seeking. ("You know you will never be satisfied here among these people.") Seven of Nine, in response, chides the Think Tank for its lack of principles: "Acquiring knowledge is a worthy objective, but its pursuit has obviously not elevated you."

"Future's End"

"Future's End" takes place in the late twentieth century—the year 1996. The action of this episode centers on Henry Starling (Ed Begley, Jr.). By the time Voyager comes into contact with Starling he is a very wealthy technology wizard, like Steve Jobs and Bill Gates. ("Our Mister Starling has built himself quite a corporate empire. Looks like he's got wealth, celebrity and an ego to match.") Starling is only able to introduce "breakthrough" technologies to the twentieth century because years earlier (in 1967) he came upon a space ship from the future. Over time Starling was able to pilfer technology from the ship.

Voyager's mission in "Future's End" is to discover why a ship from 1996 sought to travel in time, thereby destroying Earth's solar system in the twenty-ninth century. We learn that it will be Starling that will destroy the solar system when he to tries to go to the twenty-ninth century to retrieve more "new" technology for his commercial ventures. He is no longer able to extract usable technology from the ship he found years earlier. ("I've cannibalized the ship itself as much as I can. There's nothing left to base a commercial product on.")

Janeway warns Starling that his attempt to travel into the future will lead to massive catastrophe. Starling, nevertheless, is determined to pursue his goal—"will to power." Janeway rebukes Starling for his lack of ethics: "You'd destroy an entire city? [Starling threatens to destroy present-day Los Angeles if Janeway tries to stop him.] You don't care about the future, you don't care about the present. Does anything matter to you, Mister Starling?" Starling feels justified in his means and the risk he is creating because his goal is "The betterment of mankind." More specifically, he is driven by technological advancement (at least for his time period):

> My products benefit the entire world. Without me there would be no laptops, no internet, no barcode readers. What's good for Chronowerx [Starling's company] is good for everybody. I can't stop now. One trip to the twenty-ninth century and I can bring back enough technology to start the next ten computer revolutions.
>
> Janeway: In my time, Mister Starling, no human being would dream of endangering the future to gain advantage in the present.

In response, Starling takes an openly pragmatic stance (i.e., centered on the short-term): "Captain, the future you're talking about, that's nine hundred years from now. I can't be concerned about that right now. I have a company to run and a whole world full of people waiting for me to make their lives a little bit better." Voyager destroys Starling and his ship.

One cannot help but of think of the fact that U.S. capitalists (particularly in the energy sector) overtly oppose regulating greenhouse gas emissions, in spite of the escalating global devastation being brought about by climate change.[23] Corporate leaders in the U.S. energy sector seemingly adopt Starling's amazingly callous stance with regard to global warming: "Global warming is about the future, we can't be concerned about that right now. We have companies to run and a whole world full of people waiting for us to make their lives a little bit better."[24]

CONCLUSION

Popular culture, *Breaking Bad* in particular, lends significant analytical insight into the installation of Donald J. Trump as U.S. president in 2017. Trump is sharply critical of the global neoliberalist economic regime. Following from *Breaking Bad*, Trump's political, electoral draw was the fact that neoliberalism has undermined social mobility and consigned large numbers to low-paying, dead-end jobs. Perhaps just as salient is the fact that neoliberalism rewards those elites that disregard morality and ethics.

Trump, in critiquing neoliberalism, adopts the stance of a hyper-nationalist. Thus, he promises to *will to power* America's economy, along with its global authority. *Breaking Bad* indicates that *will-to-power* politics are inherently unstable and dangerous. *Star Trek* (original series) makes this precise point—even invoking the Nietzchean term of *Supermen*. Later Star Trek provides the example of the Xindi—which was destroyed by the planet's inhabitants as they (among themselves) vied for dominance.

Star Trek: Voyager episode "The Void" contains an explicit counterargument to the *will-to-power* argument. Namely, far from handicapping or undermining efficaciousness. ethics, and morality are central to success. The key to success is not the *will to power* (i.e., acting in spite of morality, ethics) but in the building of social and political capital. Such capital can only be attained through honesty and integrity, which in turn results in solidarity and collaboration. *Voyager* offers the further argument that a milieu of immorality leads to various social, political dysfunctions: pernicious *intersubjective agreements*, skulduggery, and profit-making at all costs (even global warming).

NOTES

1. Peter Baker, "'You Know What I Am? I'm a Nationalist,'" *New York Times* October 24, 2018, A12; Hall Gardner, *World War Trump: The Risks of America's New Nationalism* (Amherst, NY: Prometheus Books, 2018).

2. Joseph E. Stiglitz, *Globalization and Its Discontents Revisited: Anti-Globalization in the Era of Trump* (New York: W. W. Norton, 2017); Peter S. Goodman. "Chief of W.T.O. Worries about Its Role as Peacekeeper as a Trade War Brews," *New York Times*, March 24, 2018, A9; Steven Erlanger, "Is U.S. Foreign Policy Reverting the World to a Dark 'Jungle'?" *New York Times*, September 23, 2018, A8.

3. Gerard Huiskamp, Nick Dorzweiler, and Eli Lovely, "Watching War Movies in Baghdad: Popular Culture and the Construction of Military Policy in the Iraq War," *Polity*, 48, no. 4 (October 2016): 496–523.

4. Presaging the Trump phenomenon, in *The Politics of Star Trek: Justice, War, and the Future* (New York: Palgrave Macmillan, 2015) I wrote the following: "Globalism (modernism) in the absence of the social justice politics of the New Deal or Soviet 'socialism' prompts cynicism and a turn to traditionalism (i.e., nationalism) by communities, in part, to protect themselves from what amounts to socially, politically corrosive neoliberalism" (186).

5. Carol Diethe, *Nietzsche's Sister and the Will to Power: A Biography of Elisabeth Förster-Nietzsche* (Urbana: University of Illinois Press, 2003); David R. Koepsell and Robert Arp, eds., *Breaking Bad and Philosophy* (Chicago: Open Court, 2012).

6. Brian Leiter, *Nietzsche on Morality* (New York: Routledge, 2015).

7. Andrew J. Cherlin, *Labor's Love Lost: The Rise and Fall of the Working-Class Family in America* (Baltimore: Johns Hopkins University Press, 2014); Susan Chira, "Men Need Help. Is Hillary Clinton the Answer?" *New York Times*, October 23, 2016, SR6.

8. Abby Goodnough, "Call for Action, Not More Study, On Opioid Crisis," *New York Times*, June 17, 2017, A16; Frances Robles, "Meth, Cheaper and Deadlier, Is Surging Back," *New York Times*, February 14, 2018, A1.

9. Bruce Detwiler, *Nietzsche and the Politics of Aristocratic Radicalism* (Chicago: University of Chicago Press, 1990).

10. Mary Elizabeth Gallagher, *Contagious Capitalism: Globalization and the Politics of Labor in China* (Princeton: Princeton University Press, 2005); Kelly Sims Gallagher, *China Shifts Gears: Automakers, Oil, Pollution, and Development* (Cambridge, MA: MIT Press, 2006); Louis Uchitelle, "Goodbye, Production (and Maybe Innovation)," *New York Times*, December 24, 2006, sec. 3, p. 4; Peter S. Goodman, "U.S. and Global Economies Slipping in Unison," *New York Times*, August 24, 3008, A1; David Koistinen, *Confronting Decline: The Political Economy of Deindustrialization in Twentieth-Century New England* (Gainesville: University Press of Florida, 2013); Neil Irwin, "It's an Odd Time to Fight Globalization," *New York Times*, March 25, 2018, BU4.

11. Susan M. Wachter and Kimberly A. Zeuli, eds., *Revitalizing American Cities* (Philadelphia: University of Pennsylvania Press, 2013); Monica Davey, "A Picture of Detroit Ruin, Street by Forlorn Street," *New York Times*, February 18, 2014, A1; Jon Hurdle, "Philadelphia Forges Plan to Rebuild from Decay," *New York Times*, January 1, 2014, B1.

12. John F. Burns, "U.N. Panel to Assess Drone Use," *New York Times*, January 25, 2013, A4; Lloyd C. Gardner, *Killing Machine: The American Presidency in the Age of Drone Warfare* (New York: New Press, 2013); Thom Shanker, "Simple, Low-Cost Drones a Boost for U.S. Military," *New York Times*, January 25, 2013, A12; Declan Walsh and Ihsanullah Tipu Mehsud, "Civilian Deaths in Drone Strikes Cited in Report," *New York Times*, October 22, 2013, A1; Christopher Drew and Dave Philipps, "Burnout Forces U.S. to Curtail Drone Flights," *New York Times*, June 17, 2015, A1.

13. Detwiler, *Nietzsche and the Politics of Aristocratic Radicalism*.

14. (*Star Trek*, original series—"Space Seed" 1967).

15. David E. Sanger and Gardiner Harris, "President Reshapes Team, Hoping World Will Bend," *New York Times*, March 25, 2018, A1.

16. Jason Horowitz, "Fascists Too Lax for a Philosopher Cited by Bannon," *New York Times*, February 12, 2017, A17.

17. As quoted in Mark Landler, "Reshaping U.S. Role With One Word," *New York Times*, September 20, 2017, A1. See also Mark Landler, "Insurgent President Is Changing, Unpredictably, U.S. Global Role," *New York Times*, December 29, 2017, A1.

18. Daniel A. Gross, "'Deutschland über Alles' and 'America First,' in Song," *New Yorker*, February 18, 2017. Web.

19. Jane Caplan, *Nazi Germany (Short Oxford History of Germany)* (New York: Oxford University Press, 2008); Michael Cowan, *Cult of the Will: Nervousness and German Modernity* (University Park: Penn State University Press, 2013).

20. Michael Walzer, *Thinking Politically: Essays in Political Theory*, David Miller ed. (New Haven: Yale University Press, 2007), chap. 1.

21. Daniel H. Nexon and Iver B. Neuman, *Harry Potter and International Relations* (Lanham, MD: Rowman & Littlefield, 2006); Daniel W. Drezner, *Theories of International Politics and Zombies* (Princeton: Princeton University Press, 2011); Jason Dittmer, *Captain America and the Nationalist Superhero* (Philadelphia: Temple University Press, 2012).

22. Richard Rorty, writing in the early 1980s, argues that societies are based on *intersubjective agreement*. Thus, what is required for societal stability is enough consensus on a set of ideas—any set of ideas. Hence, what matters is consensus, and not the ideas themselves. Richard Rorty, *Philosophy and the Mirror of Nature* (Princeton: Princeton University Press, 1981); Michael Bacon, *Richard Rorty: Pragmatism and Political Liberalism* (Lanham: Lexington Books, 2007); Neil Gross, *Richard Rorty: The Making of an American Philosopher* (Chicago: University of Chicago Press, 2008).

23. George A. Gonzalez, *Energy and Empire: The Politics of Nuclear and Solar Power in the United States* (Albany: State University of New York Press, 2012), *American Empire and the Canadian Oil Sands* (New York: Palgrave MacMillan, 2016), and *Energy, the Modern State, and the American World System* (Albany: State University New York Press, 2018).

24. For instance, Lisa Friedman, "How a Coal Baron's Wish List Became Trump's To-Do List," *New York Times*, January 10, 2018, B1.

Conclusion

Popular Culture and Reasons in the World

This volume opened with the argument that normative values metaphysically exist—as part of the Hegelian *Absolute* (introduction). The Absolute results in the moral, ethical, and political reasons in the world. Put differently, people act in response to the normative values (*spirits*) of the Absolute. Some of these values are broadly perceived as positive (love, altruism, friendliness, and so on), while others are deemed negative (selfishness, vanity, narcissism, and so forth).

The prime argument of this book is that the public gains analytical understanding of the political reasons in the world through art—particularly popular art of high quality. I have especially focused on the hugely popular broadcast iterations of the Star Trek franchise to analyze society's political values and the public's understanding of the political reasoning of elites. Relying on movies and television (popular culture), we can arguably grasp the political and social implications of predicating the global economy (neoliberalism) on the *spirit* of acquisitiveness (i.e., greed). By giving a green light (so to speak) to greed, society is ostensibly fostering the pathology of wealth addiction—particularly among the economic elite, which on its face is profoundly dangerous for society and the biosphere. I also outline in chapter 1 how the Star Trek franchise posits the progressive dialectic—the historical process of humanity moving through revolutionary events toward the ideal (utopia) of a classless society, free of gender and ethnic biases. The progressive dialectic is propelled forward by the normative values of social justice, truth, and scientific and intellectual discovery.

Chapter 2 is dedicated to treating analytic philosophy. Analytic philosophers base their thinking exclusively on material reality—denying the metaphysical existence of normative values (e.g., justice). By focusing entirely on material reality and eliding normative values, analytic philosophers reject art as a source of knowledge of reason in the world. Taking it a step further, analytic philosophy seeks to actively elide the normative values embedded in art (e.g., Star Trek).

Very importantly, a focus only on material reality (*material realism*) prevents analytic philosophy from developing a coherent, convincing theory of the mind. As a result, analytic philosophy is not useful in philosophizing or speculating about such debilitating afflictions of the mind, memory as PTSD (post-traumatic stress disorder) (chapter 5). Hegelian theory indicates that PTSD results from the knowledge, indelible recollection of acting heinously (murder, torture) against the progressive dialectic. These evil acts are embedded in the Absolute. Additionally, analytic philosophy is not helpful in cogitating the question of the intellectual autonomy or subservience of sentient clones (more specifically cloned warriors) (chapter 6). Again drawing on Hegelian thought, to be sentient is to have an autonomous relationship to the Absolute and the normative reasons in the world.

Judging from the depiction of Abraham Lincoln in the original *Star Trek* series "Savage Curtain" (chapter 3), the sixteenth president of the United States continues to be greatly admired on a worldwide basis. As a result of his committed leadership of the Northern Cause in defeating the Southern slavocracy, Lincoln is the embodiment of the progressive values of free labor, democratic governance, and racial fairness. Contrary to the arguments of André M. Carrington and Daniel Bernardi, the popularity of the Star Trek franchise should be read as the public's broad commitment to ethnic equality (an explicit rejection of the politics of *the other*) (chapter 4).

Beginning in the 1990s, the creators of *Deep Space Nine* began warning of trends and elite machinations toward authoritarianism. The series saliently pointed to the "state within the state" phenomenon in the developed world (Section 31)—today, publicly referred to as the "Deep State." Later television series expound upon the Deep State—with *Justice League Unlimited* positing the *state-within-the-state* organization of *Cadmus* (acting outside of Congressional oversight). *The Blacklist* in the contemporary period has the secretive and morally bankrupt Cabal, led by economic elites and other criminal elements, acting as the prime architects of the world system. With important aspects of the government beyond public view and completely disregarding the law, the president in *House of Cards* also operates in the shadows without any scruples whatsoever (chapter 7). The themes that run through these shows indicate that the public is cynical about government and (un)democratic practices within the *neoliberlist world system*.

This cynicism informs the series *Breaking Bad* and arguably the installation of Donald J. Trump as U.S. president (chapter 8). Apart from government, international corporate behemoths act without morals—cold heartedly divesting from communities to devastating effects as a matter of course. The profit motive (*greed addiction*) of the Billionaire Class creates a global milieu where elites act entirely on the *will to power*. The political figure of Trump represents the rejection of this neoliberalist (amoral) milieu, and at the same time replicates its politics by promising to *will to power* the U.S. state and economy (total global hegemony). Somewhat paradoxically, only the unscrupulous can succeed within a worldwide politics where morality, ethics has no currency. Walter White of *Breaking Bad* only excels and thrives by embracing this precise reality.

Going back to the Star Trek of the 1960s, the original series expressly critiqued the Nietzschean politics of *radical aristocracy*—denouncing the very concept of *Supermen* as inherently warmongering and globally destructive. The *Voyager* episode "The Void" serves as a clear-throated rejection of *will-to-power* ethics—in this episode, the idea that consensus building and solidarity (a seeming rejection of the political values of neoliberalism) are the only means to success is lucidly and convincingly depicted.

Bibliography

"About Those Black Sites," *New York Times*, February 18, 2013, A16.
"After the Attacks: Bush's Remarks to Cabinet and Advisers," *New York Times*, September 13, 2001. Web.
Alderman, Liz. "Humans Wanted, But Robots Work," *New York Times*, April 17, 2018, B1.
Ambinder, Marc, and D. B. Grady. *Deep State: Inside the Government Secrecy Industry* (Hoboken, NJ: Wiley, 2013).
Anderegg, Michael, ed. *Inventing Vietnam: The War in Film and Television* (Philadelphia: Temple University Press, 1991).
Anderson, Terry H. *Bush's Wars* (New York: Oxford University Press, 2011).
Arrighi, Giovanni, with Beverly Silver. *Chaos and Governance in the Modern World System* (Minneapolis: University of Minnesota Press, 1999).
Bacon, Michael. *Richard Rorty: Pragmatism and Political Liberalism* (Lanham: Lexington Books, 2007).
Baker, Peter. "You Know What I Am? I'm a Nationalist." *New York Times*. October 24, 2018, A12.
Balint, Benjamin. *Running Commentary: The Contentious Magazine That Transformed the Jewish Left into the Neoconservative Right* (New York: Public Affairs, 2010).
Barilleaux, Ryan J., and Christopher S. Kelley, eds. *The Unitary Executive and the Modern Presidency* (College Station: Texas A&M University Press, 2010).
Barrow, Clyde W. *Critical Theories of the State* (Madison: University of Wisconsin Press, 1993).
Barrow, Clyde W. *Toward a Critical Theory of States: The Poulantzas-Miliband Debate after Globalization.* Albany: State University of New York Press, 2016.
Bates, Jennifer Ann. *Hegel's Theory of Imagination* (Albany: State University of New York Press, 2004).
Bendersky, Joseph W. *Carl Schmitt: Theorist for the Reich* (Princeton: Princeton University Press, 1983).
Bernardi, Daniel Leonard. *Star Trek and History: Race-ing toward a White Future* (New Brunswick, NJ: Rutgers University Press, 1998).
Bernasek, Anna. "The Typical Household, Now Worth A Third Less," *New York Times*, July 27, 2014, BU6.
Blue Bloods—"School of Hard Knocks" (2018).

Booker, Keith M. "The Politics of Star Trek," in *The Essential Science Fiction Reader*, J.P. Telotte, ed. (Lexington: University Press of Kentucky, 2008).
Bowman, Brady. *Hegel and the Metaphysics of Absolute Negativity* (Cambridge: Cambridge University Press, 2015).
Breaking Bad—"Caballo sin Nombre" (2010).
Breaking Bad—"Cornered" (2011).
Breaking Bad—"Face Off" (2011).
Breaking Bad—"Pilot" (2008).
Bronner, Stephen Eric. *Rosa Luxemburg: A Revolutionary for Our Times* (University Park: Pennsylvania State University Press, 1993).
Cannon, James P. *The History of American Trotskyism: Report of a Participant* (New York: Pioneer Publishers, 1944).
Caplan, Jane. *Nazi Germany (Short Oxford History of Germany)* (New York: Oxford University Press, 2008).
Carrington, André M. *Speculative Blackness: The Future of Race in Science Fiction* (Minneapolis: University of Minnesota Press, 2016).
Carwardine, Richard, and Jay Sexton, eds. *The Global Lincoln* (New York: Oxford University Press, 2011).
Cherlin, Andrew J. *Labor's Love Lost: The Rise and Fall of the Working-Class Family in America* (Baltimore: Johns Hopkins University Press, 2014).
Chidester, Jeffrey L., and Paul Kengor, eds. *Reagan's Legacy in a World Transformed* (Cambridge, MA: Harvard University Press, 2015).
Childs, Peter. *Modernism* (New York: Routledge, 2007).
Chira, Susan. "Men Need Help. Is Hillary Clinton the Answer?" *New York Times*, October 23, 2016, SR6.
Chokshi, Niraj. "Robot Cures Human Headache: Putting Together Ikea Furniture," *New York Times*, April 19, 2018, B8.
Chomsky, Noam. *Language and Mind*, 3rd ed. (New York: Cambridge University Press, 2006).
Cohen, Patricia. "Study Finds Global Wealth Is Flowing to the Richest," *New York Times*, January 19, 2015, B6.
Colaresi, Michael P. *Democracy Declassified: The Secrecy Dilemma in National Security* (New York: Oxford University Press, 2014).
Connor, Steven. "Doing without Art," *New Literary History* 42, no. 1: 53–69.
Cowan, Michael. *Cult of the Will: Nervousness and German Modernity* (University Park: Penn State University Press, 2013).
Dahl, Robert A., and Charles E. Lindblom. "Preface" in *Politics, Economics, and Welfare* (New Haven, CT: Yale University Press, 1976).
Dallek, Robert. *Lyndon B. Johnson: Portrait of a President* (New York: Oxford University Press, 2005.
"Dark Again after the Torture Report," *New York Times*, December 12, 2014, A34.
Davey, Monica. "A Picture of Detroit Ruin, Street by Forlorn Street," *New York Times*, February 18., 2014, A1.
Davis, Julie Hirschfeld. "'Deep State'? Until Now, It Was a Foreign Concept," *New York Times*, March 7, 2017, A19.
de Lagasnerie, Geoffroy. *The Art of Revolt: Snowden, Assange, Manning* (Stanford: Stanford University Press, 2017).
Desmond, William. *Art and the Absolute: A Study of Hegel's Aesthetics* (Albany: State University of New York Press, 1986).
Detwiler, Bruce. *Nietzsche and the Politics of Aristocratic Radicalism* (Chicago: University of Chicago Press, 1990).
Dewan, Shaila, and Robert Gebeloff. "One Percent, Many Variations," *New York Times*, January 15, 2012, A1.
Dickie, John. *Cosa Nostra: A History of the Sicilian Mafia* (New York: Palgrave Macmillan, 2005).
Diethe, Carol. *Nietzsche's Sister and the Will to Power: A Biography of Elisabeth Förster-Nietzsche* (Urbana: University of Illinois Press, 2003).

Dittmer, Jason. *Captain America and the Nationalist Superhero* (Philadelphia: Temple University Press, 2012).
Domenig, Christian. "Klingons: Going Medieval on You," in *Star Trek and History*, Nancy R. Reagin, ed. (Hoboken, NJ: John Wiley & Sons, 2013).
Domhoff, G. William. *Who Rules America?*, 7th ed. (New York: McGraw-Hill, 2014).
Dorrien, Gary. *The Neoconservative Mind: Politics, Culture, and the War of Ideology* (Philadelphia: Temple University Press, 1993).
Dorrien, Gary. *Imperial Designs: Neoconservatism and the New Pax Americana* (New York: Routledge, 2004).
Drape, Joe. "Bankruptcy for Ailing Detroit, but Prosperity for Its Teams," *New York Times*, October 14, 2013, A1.
Drezner, Daniel W. *Theories of International Politics and Zombies* (Princeton: Princeton University Press, 2011).
Drolet, Jean-François. *American Neoconservatism: The Politics and Culture of a Reactionary Idealism* (New York: Columbia University Press, 2011).
Drury, Shadia B. *Leo Strauss and the American Right* (New York: St. Martin's Press, 1997).
Duménil, Gérard, and Dominique Lévy. *Capital Resurgent: Roots of the Neoliberal Revolution*, trans. Derek Jeffers (Cambridge, MA: Harvard University Press, 2004).
Eberl, Jason T. and Kevin S. Decker, eds. *Star Trek and Philosophy: The Wrath of Kant* (Chicago: Open Court, 2008).
Ede, Siân. *Art and Science* (New York: I. B. Tauris, 2005).
"Effort to Prohibit Waterboarding Fails in House," Associated Press. March 12, 2008. Web.
Ehrman, John. *The Rise of Neoconservatism: Intellectuals and Foreign Affairs, 1945–1994* (New York: Cambridge University Press, 1995).
Eldridge, Richard. *Beyond Representation: Philosophy and Poetic Imagination* (New York: Cambridge University Press, 2011).
Erlanger, Steven. "Is U.S. Foreign Policy Reverting the World to a Dark 'Jungle'?" *New York Times*, September 23, 2018, A8.
Fandos, Nicholas, and Sharon LaFraniere. "Two Reports on Meddling: Choose Your Own Verdict," *New York Times*, April 28, 2018, A14.
Feenberg, Andrew. *Technosystem: The Social Life of Reason* (Cambridge, MA: Harvard University Press, 2017).
Fields, A. Belden. *Trotskyism and Maoism: Theory and Practice in France and the United States* (New York: Praeger, 1988).
Flegenheimer, Matt, and Scott Shane. "Bipartisan Voices Back U.S. Agencies on Russia Hacking," *New York Times*, January 6, 2017, A1.
Frank, Adam. "Is a Climate Disaster Inevitable?" *New York Times*, January 18, 2015, SR6.
Frank, Robert. "Another Widening Gap: The Haves vs. the Have-Mores," *New York Times*, November 16, 2014, BU4.
Friedman, Lisa. "How a Coal Baron's Wish List Became Trump's To-Do List," *New York Times*, January 10, 2018, B1.
Friedman, Murray. *The Neoconservative Revolution: Jewish Intellectuals and the Shaping of Public Policy* (New York: Cambridge University Press, 2005).
Frölich, Paul. *Rosa Luxemburg: Her Life and Work* (New York: Howard Fertig, 1969).
Gallagher, Kelly Sims. *China Shifts Gears: Automakers, Oil, Pollution, and Development* (Cambridge, MA: MIT Press, 2006).
Gallagher, Mary Elizabeth. *Contagious Capitalism: Globalization and the Politics of Labor in China* (Princeton: Princeton University Press, 2005).
Gardner, Hall. *World War Trump: The Risks of America's New Nationalism* (Amherst, NY: Prometheus Books, 2018).
George, Roger Z., and Harvey Rishikoff. *The National Security Enterprise: Navigating the Labyrinth* (Washington D.C.: Georgetown University Press, 2011).
Giglio, James N. *The Presidency of John F. Kennedy* (Lawrence: University of Kansas Press, 2006).
Gilman, Nils. *Mandarins of the Future: Modernization Theory in Cold War America* (Baltimore, MD: Johns Hopkins University Press, 2007).

Glock, Hans-Johann. *What Is Analytic Philosophy?* (New York: Cambridge University Press, 2008).
Goldberg, Michelle. "Trump Shows the World He's Putin's Lackey," *New York Times*, July 17, 2018, A21.
Goldman, Adam, Michael S. Schmidt, and Nicholas Fandos. "F.B.I. Investigated if Trump Worked for the Russians," *New York Times*, January 12, 2019, A1.
Gonzalez, George A. *Urban Sprawl, Global Warming, and the Empire of Capital* (Albany: State University of New York Press, 2009).
Gonzalez, George A. *Energy and Empire: The Politics of Nuclear and Solar Power in the United States* (Albany: State University of New York Press, 2012).
Gonzalez, George A. *The Politics of Star Trek: Justice, War, and the Future* (New York: Palgrave MacMillan, 2015).
Gonzalez, George A. *American Empire and the Canadian Oil Sands* (New York: Palgrave MacMillan, 2016).
Gonzalez, George A. "*Justice League Unlimited* and the Politics of Globalization." *Foundation: The International Review of Science Fiction* 45, no. 123 (2016): 5–13.
Gonzalez, George A. *The Absolute and Star Trek* (New York: Palgrave Macmillan, 2017).
Gonzalez, George A. *Star Trek and the Politics of Globalism* (New York: Palgrave Macmillan, 2018).
Goodman, Peter S. "U.S. and Global Economies Slipping in Unison," *New York Times*, August 24, 2008, A1.
Goodman, Peter S. "Sweden Adds Human Touch to a Robotic Future," *New York Times*, December 28, 2017, A1.
Goodman, Peter S. "Chief of W.T.O. Worries about Its Role as Peacekeeper as a Trade War Brews," *New York Times*, March 24, 2018, A9.
Goodnough, Abby. "Call for Action, Not More Study, On Opioid Crisis," *New York Times*, June 17, 2017, A16.
Gordon, Paul. *Art as the Absolute: Art's Relation to Metaphysics in Kant, Fichte, Schelling, Hegel, and Schopenhauer* (New York: Bloomsbury Academic, 2015).
Gross, Daniel A. "'Deutschland über Alles' and 'America First,' in Song," *New Yorker*, February 18, 2017. Web.
Gross, Neil. *Richard Rorty: The Making of an American Philosopher* (Chicago: University of Chicago Press, 2008).
Hall, Martin, and Patrick Thaddeus Jackson, eds. *Civilization Identity* (New York: Palgrave Macmillan, 2007).
Hanley, Richard. *The Metaphysics of Star Trek* (New York: Basic, 1997).
Haverty-Stacke, Donna T. *Trotskyists on Trial: Free Speech and Political Persecution since the Age of FDR* (New York: New York University Press, 2016).
Hazony, Yoram. *The Virtue of Nationalism* (New York: Basic, 2018).
Hodgson, Godfrey. *JFK and LBJ: The Last Two Great Presidents* (New Haven: Yale University Press, 2015).
Hook, Sidney. *Towards the Understanding of Karl Marx* (New York: John Day, 1933).
Horkheimer, Max. *Critique of Instrumental Reason*, trans. Matthew O'Connell (New York: Verso, 2013).
Horowitz, Jason. "Fascists Too Lax for a Philosopher Cited by Bannon," *New York Times*, February 12, 2017, A17.
Houlgate, Stephen. *Hegel's "Phenomenology of Spirit": A Reader's Guide* (New York: Bloomsbury Academic, 2013).
Huiskamp, Gerard, Nick Dorzweiler, and Eli Lovely. "Watching War Movies in Baghdad: Popular Culture and the Construction of Military Policy in the Iraq War," *Polity* 48, no. 4 (October 2016): 496–523.
Huntington, Samuel P. *The Clash of Civilizations and the Remaking of World Order* (New York: Simon & Schuster, 1996).
Hurdle, Jon. "Philadelphia Forges Plan to Rebuild from Decay," *New York Times*, January 1, 2014, B1.

Ingraham, Christopher. "The Richest 1 Percent Now Owns More of the Country's Wealth Than at Any Time in the Past 50 Years," *Washington Post*, December 6, 2017. Web.
Irwin, Neil. "Economic Expansion for Everyone? Not Anymore," *New York Times*, September 27, 2014, B1.
Ismael, Jacqueline S. *Kuwait: Dependency and Class in a Rentier State* (Gainesville: University of Florida Press, 1993).
Jeffers, Thomas L. *Norman Podhoretz: A Biography* (New York: Cambridge University Press, 2010).
Jones, Daniel Stedman. *Masters of the Universe: Hayek, Friedman, and the Birth of Neoliberal Politics* (Princeton: Princeton University Press, 2012).
Justice League Unlimited—"Flashpoint" (2005).
Justice League Unlimited—"Question Authority" (2005).
Justice League Unlimited—"The Doomsday Sanction" (2005).
Justice League Unlimited—"The Ties That Bind" (2005).
Justice League Unlimited—"To Another Shore" (2005).
Kading, Terry. "Drawn into 9/11, but Where Have All the Superheroes Gone?," in Jeff McLaughlin, ed. *Comics as Philosophy* (Jackson: University of Mississippi, 2005).
Kaminsky, Jack. *Hegel on Art: An Interpretation of Hegel's Aesthetics* (Albany: State University of New York Press, 1962).
Kant, Immanuel. *Critique of Pure Reason*, trans. Max Muller (New York: Penguin, 2008 [1781]).
Kemp, Martin. *Seen | Unseen: Art, Science, and Intuition from Leonardo to the Hubble Telescope* (New York: Oxford University Press, 2006).
Kerbo, Harold. *World Poverty: The Roots of Global Inequality and the Modern World System* (New York: McGraw-Hill, 2005).
Klein, Gérard. "From the Images of Science to Science Fiction," in *Learning from Other Worlds*, Patrick Parrinder, ed. (Durham, NC: Duke University Press, 2001).
Klotzko, Arlene Judith. *A Clone of Your Own?* (New York: Cambridge University Press, 2006).
Koepsell, David R., and Robert Arp, eds. *Breaking Bad and Philosophy* (Chicago: Open Court, 2012).
Koistinen, David. *Confronting Decline: The Political Economy of Deindustrialization in Twentieth-Century New England* (Gainesville: University Press of Florida, 2013).
Kotsko, Adam. *Neoliberalism's Demons: On the Political Theology of Late Capital* (Stanford University Press, 2018).
Kreines, James. *Reason in the World: Hegel's Metaphysics and its Philosophical Appeal* (New York: Oxford University Press, 2015).
Kristof, Nicholas. "An Idiot's Guide to Inequality," *New York Times*, July 24, 2014, A27.
Krugman, Paul. "Oligarchy, American Style," *New York Times*, November 4, 2011, A31.
Krugman, Paul. "Robots and Robber Barons," *New York Times*, December 10, 2012, A27.
Krugman, Paul, "The Undeserving Rich," *New York Times*, January 20, 2014, A17.
Lagon, Mark P. "'We Owe It to Them to Interfere:' *Star Trek* and U.S. Statecraft in the 1960s and the 1990s," in *Political Science Fiction*, Donald M. Hassler and Clyde Wilcox, eds. (Columbia: University of South Carolina Press, 1997).
Landler, Mark. "Reshaping U.S. Role with One Word," *New York Times*, September 20, 2017, A1.
Landler, Mark. "Insurgent President Is Changing, Unpredictably, U.S. Global Role," *New York Times*, December 29, 2017, A1.
Latham, Michael E. *Modernization as Ideology: American Social Science and "Nation Building" in the Kennedy Era* (University of North Carolina Press, 2000).
Latham, Michael E. *The Right Kind of Revolution: Modernization, Development, and U.S. Foreign Policy from the Cold War to the Present* (Cornell University Press, 2010).
Leiter, Brian. *Nietzsche on Morality* (New York: Routledge, 2015).
Leonhardt, David. "All for the 1%, 1% for All," *New York Times*, May 4, 2014, MM23.
Leonhardt, David. "We're Measuring the Economy All Wrong," *New York Times*, September 14, 2018. Web.

Levick, Stephen E. *Clone Being: Exploring the Psychological and Social Dimensions* (Lanham, MD: Rowman & Littlefield, 2003).
Levine, Lawrence. *Highbrow/Lowbrow: The Emergence of Cultural Hierarchy in America* (Cambridge, MA: Harvard University Press, 1990).
Lucifer—"#TeamLucifer" (2016).
Mahler, Jonathan. "After the Imperial Presidency," *New York Times Magazine*, November 9, 2008, MM42.
Maker, William, ed. *Hegel and Aesthetics* (Albany: State University of New York Press, 2000).
Manjoo, Farhad. "Uber's Business Model Could Change Your Work," *New York Times*, January 29, 2015, B1.
Marx, Karl. *On the Jewish Question*. 1844. Web.
Marx, Karl. *The Critique of the Gotha Programme* (London: Electric Book Co., 2001 [1875]). Web.
Mazzetti, Mark. "Panel Faults C.I.A. over Brutality toward Terrorism Suspects," *New York Times*, December 10, 2014, A1.
McCumber, John. *Time in a Ditch: American Philosophy in the McCarthy Era* (Evanston, IL: Northwestern University Press, 2001).
McCumber, John. *The Philosophy Scare: The Politics of Reason in the Early Cold War*. (Chicago: University of Chicago Press, 2016).
McGilvray, James. *Chomsky: Language, Mind, and Politics* (Cambridge: Polity, 1999).
McIntire, Mike. "Nonprofit Acts as a Stealth Business Lobbyist," *New York Times*, April 22, 2012, A1.
McKee, Guin A. *The Problem of Jobs: Liberalism, Race, and Deindustrialization in Philadelphia* (Chicago: University of Chicago Press, 2009).
McLaren, Darcee L., and Jennifer E. Porter. "(Re)Covering Sacred Ground: New Age Spirituality in Star Trek: *Voyager*," in *Star Trek and Sacred Ground: Explorations of Star Trek, Religion, and American Culture*, Jennifer E. Porter and Darcee L. McLaren, ed. (Albany: State University of New York Press, 1999).
McPherson, James M. *Abraham Lincoln and the Second American Revolution* (New York: Oxford University Press, 1992).
Menand, Louis. *The Metaphysical Club* (New York: Farrar, Straus, and Giroux, 2001).
Miller, Claire Cain. "Smarter Robots Move Deeper into Workplace," *New York Times*, December 16, 2014, A1.
Miller, Claire Cain. "What's Really Killing Jobs? It's Automation, Not China," *New York Times*, December 22, 2016, A3.
Miller, Carol Poh, and Robert Wheeler. *Cleveland: A Concise History* (Bloomington: Indiana University Press, 2009).
"Mr. Trump and Mr. Putin, Best Frenemies," *New York Times*, June 29, 2018, A26.
Mumford, Stephen. *Metaphysics: A Very Short Introduction* (New York: New York: Oxford University Press, 2012).
Myers, Constance Ashton. *The Prophet's Army: Trotskyists in America, 1928–1941* (Westport, CT: Greenwood Press, 1977).
Nanay, Bence. *Aesthetics as Philosophy of Perception* (New York: Oxford University Press, 2016).
Natta, Jr., Don Van, Adam Liptak and Clifford J. Levy. "The Miller Case: A Notebook, A Cause, a Jail Cell and a Deal," *New York Times*, October 16, 2005, sec. 1, p. 1.
Nexon, Daniel H, and Iver B. Neuman. *Harry Potter and International Relations* (Lanham, MD: Rowman & Littlefield, 2006).
Norton, Anne. *Leo Strauss and the Politics of American Empire* (New Haven: Yale University Press, 2004).
Oakes, James. *Freedom National: The Destruction of Slavery in the United States* (New York: W.W. Norton & Company, 2012).
Osborn, Ronald E. *Humanism and the Death of God: Searching for the Good after Darwin, Marx, and Nietzsche* (New York: Oxford University Press, 2017).

Padgett, Deborah K., Benjamin F. Henwood, and Sam J. Tsemberis. *Housing First: Ending Homelessness, Transforming Systems, and Changing Lives* (New York: Oxford University Press, 2015).
Palmer, Bryan D. *James P. Cannon and the Origins of the American Revolutionary Left, 1890–1928* (Urbana: University of Illinois Press, 2010).
Paoli, Letizia. *Mafia Brotherhoods: Organized Crime, Italian Style* (New York: Oxford University Press, 2008).
Paolucci, Henry. "Introduction" in *Hegel: On the Arts*, Henry Paolucci, ed., 2nd ed. (Smyrna, DE: Griffon House, 2001).
Parr, Adrian. *The Wrath of Capital: Neoliberalism and Climate Change Politics* (New York: Columbia University Press, 2013).
Piketty, Thomas. *Capital in the Twenty-First Century*, trans. Arthur Goldhammer (Cambridge, MA: Belknap Press, 2014).
Pillow, Kirk. *Sublime Understanding: Aesthetic Reflection in Kant and Hegel* (Cambridge, MA: MIT Press, 2000).
Polk, Sam. "For the Love of Money." *New York Times*, January 19, 2014, SR1.
Raab, Selwyn. *Five Families: The Rise, Decline, and Resurgence of America's Most Powerful Mafia Empires* (New York: St. Martin's Griffin, 2006).
Rauchway, Eric. *The Great Depression and the New Deal: A Very Short Introduction* (New York: Oxford University Press, 2008).
"Rewriting the Geneva Conventions." *New York Times*, August 14, 2006, A20.
Reynolds, Richard. *Super Heroes: A Modern Mythology* (Jackson: University Press of Mississippi, 1992).
Risen, James. "Before Shooting in Iraq, Warning on Blackwater," *New York Times*, June 30, 2014, A1.
Risen, James. and Mark Mazetti. "Case Ends against Ex-Blackwater Officials," *New York Times*, February 22, 2013, A16.
Robles, Frances. "Meth, Cheaper and Deadlier, Is Surging Back," *New York Times*, February 14, 2018, A1.
Rockmore, Tom. *Marx's Dream: From Capitalism to Communism* (Chicago: University of Chicago Press, 2018).
Romano, Carlin. *America the Philosophical* (New York: Simon & Schuster, 2012).
Rorty, Richard. *Philosophy and the Mirror of Nature* (Princeton: Princeton University Press, 1981).
Rossinow, Doug. *The Reagan Era: A History of the 1980s* (New York: Columbia University Press, 2015).
Sanger, David E., and Gardiner Harris. "President Reshapes Team, Hoping World Will Bend," *New York Times*, March 25, 2018, A1.
Sarantakes, Nicholas Evan. "Cold War Pop Culture and the Image of U.S. Foreign Policy: The Perspective of the Original *Star Trek* of U.S. Foreign Policy," *Journal of Cold War Studies* 7, no. 4 (2005): 74–103.
Schecter, Darrow. *The Critique of Instrumental Reason from Weber to Habermas* (New York: Bloomsbury Academic, 2012).
Schmitt, Carl. *The Concept of the Political*, expanded edition (Chicago: University of Chicago University, 2007 [1929]).
Schwartz, Stephen P. *A Brief History of Analytic Philosophy: From Russell to Rawls* (West Sussex, UK: Wiley-Blackwell, 2012).
Seefedt, Kristin S., and John D. Graham. *America's Poor and the Great Recession* (Bloomington: Indiana University Press, 2013).
Shafer-Landau, Russ. *Whatever Happened to Good and Evil?* (New York: Oxford University Press, 2003).
Shane, Scott. "Waterboarding Used 266 Times on 2 Suspects," *New York Times*, April 20, 2009, A1.
Shane, Scott. "Portrayal of C.I.A. Torture in Bin Laden Film Reopens a Debate," *New York Times*, December 13, 2012, A1.

Shane, Scott. "U.S. Practiced Torture after 9/11, Nonpartisan Review Concludes," *New York Times*, April 16, 2013, A1.
Shane, Scott, and Andrew W. Lehren. "Leaked Cables Offer Raw Look at U.S. Diplomacy." *New York Times*, November 29, 2010, A1.
Shane, Scott, and Mark Mazzetti." The Plot to Subvert an Election," *New York Times*, September 20, 2018. Web.
Shapiro, Alan. *Star Trek. Technologies of Disappearance* (Berlin: Avinus Press, 2004).
Slater, Philip E. *Wealth Addiction* (New York: Dutton, 1980).
Smith, Adam. *The Wealth of Nations* (New York: Bantam, 2003 [1776]).
Snee, Brian J. *Lincoln before Lincoln* (Lexington: University of Kentucky Press, 2016).
Solnit, Rebecca. "Bird by Bird," *New York Times Magazine*, December 7, 2014, MM13.
Star Trek—"Bread and Circuses" (1968).
Star Trek—"Day of the Dove" (1968).
Star Trek—"Mirror, Mirror" (1967).
Star Trek—"Patterns of Force" (1968).
Star Trek—"Space Seed" (1967).
Star Trek—"The Apple" (1967).
Star Trek—"The Cloud Minders" (1969).
Star Trek—"The Omega Glory" (1968).
Star Trek—"The Savage Curtain" (1969).
Star Trek: Deep Space Nine—"Bar Association" (1996).
Star Trek: Deep Space Nine—"Crossover" (1994).
Star Trek: Deep Space Nine—"Defiant" (1994).
Star Trek: Deep Space Nine—"Homefront"(1996).
Star Trek: Deep Space Nine—"Improbable Cause" (1995).
Star Trek: Deep Space Nine—"In the Cards" (1997).
Star Trek: Deep Space Nine—"Inquisition" (1998).
Star Trek: Deep Space Nine—"Inter Arma Enim Silent Leges" (1999).
Star Trek: Deep Space Nine—"Little Green Men" (1995).
Star Trek: Deep Space Nine—"Past Tense" (1995).
Star Trek: Deep Space Nine—"Paradise Lost" (1996).
Star Trek: Deep Space Nine"—Prophet Motive" (1995).
Star Trek: Deep Space Nine—"The Search" (1994).
Star Trek: Deep Space Nine—"The Way of the Warrior" 1995.
Star Trek: Deep Space Nine—"When it Rains . . ." (1999).
Star Trek: Enterprise—"Anomaly" (2003).
Star Trek: Enterprise—"Fallen Hero" (2002).
Star Trek: Enterprise—"Fusion" (2002).
Star Trek: Enterprise—"In a Mirror, Darkly" (2005).
Star Trek: Enterprise—"Shadows of P'Jem" (2002).
Star Trek: Enterprise—"Stormfront" (2004).
Star Trek: Enterprise—"Terra Prime" (2005).
Star Trek: Enterprise—"The Andorian Incident" (2001).
Star Trek: Enterprise—"The Shipment" (2003).
Star Trek: First Contact (1996).
Star Trek: The Next Generation—"All Goods Things . . . " (1994).
Star Trek: The Next Generation—"Encounter at Farpoint" (1987).
Star Trek: The Next Generation—"Face of the Enemy" (1993).
Star Trek: The Next Generation—"Heart of Glory" (1988).
Star Trek: The Next Generation—"Redemption" (1991).
Star Trek: The Next Generation—"Sarek" (1992).
Star Trek: The Next Generation—"The Drumhead" (1991).
Star Trek: The Next Generation—"The First Duty" (1992).
Star Trek: The Next Generation—"The Icarus Factor" (1989).
Star Trek: The Next Generation—"The Measure of a Man" (1989).
Star Trek: The Next Generation—"The Naked Now" (1987).

Star Trek: The Next Generation—"The Neutral Zone" (1988).
Star Trek: The Next Generation—"Transfigurations" (1990).
Star Trek: Voyager—"Author, Author" (2001).
Star Trek: Voyager—"False Profits" (1996).
Star Trek: Voyager—"Future's End" (1996).
Star Trek: Voyager—"Memorial" (2000).
Star Trek: Voyager—"Phage" (1995).
Star Trek: Voyager—"Sacred Ground" (1996).
Star Trek: Voyager—"Scorpion" (1997).
Star Trek: Voyager—"The Killing Game" (1998).
Star Trek: Voyager—"Think Tank" (1999).
Star Trek: Voyager—"The Void" (2001).
Stern, David S., ed. *Essays on Hegel's Philosophy of Subjective Spirit* (Albany: State University of New York Press, 2013).
Stevenson, Richard W. "White House says Prisoner Policy Set Humane Tone," *New York Times*, June 23, 2004, A1.
Stiglitz, Joseph E. *Globalization and Its Discontents Revisited. Anti-Globalization in the Era of Trump* (New York: W.W. Norton, 2017).
Stolberg, Sheryl Gay, Nicholas Fandos, and Thomas Kaplan. "Measured Condemnation But No G.O.P. Plan to Act," *New York Times*, July 17, 2018, A1.
Sugrue, Thomas J. *The Origins of the Urban Crisis: Race and Inequality in Postwar Detroit* (Princeton: Princeton University Press, 2005).
Sweet, Derek R. *Star Wars in the Public Square: The Clone Wars as Political Dialogue* (Jefferson, NC: MacFarland, 2015).
Tabuchi, Hiroko. "The Banks Putting Rain Forests in Peril," *New York Times*, December 4, 2016, BU1.
The Blacklist—"Gina Zanetakos" (2013).
The Blacklist—"Quon Zhang" (2015).
The Blacklist—"Susan Hargrave" (2016).
"Ten States Still Have Fewer Jobs Since Recession," *Reuters*, March 25, 2016.
Thompson, C. Bradley, with Yaron Brook. *Neoconservatism: An Obituary for an Idea* (Boulder, CO: Paradigm Publishers, 2010).
Tufekci, Zeynep. "The Machines Are Coming," *New York Times*, April 19, 2015, SR4.
Uchitelle, Louis. "Goodbye, Production (and Maybe Innovation)." *New York Times*, December 24, 2006, sec. 3 p. 4.
Vaïsse, Justin. *Neoconservatism: The Biography of a Movement* (Cambridge, MA: Harvard UniversityPress, 2010).
Vegso, Roland. *The Naked Communist: Cold War Modernism and the Politics of Popular Culture* (New York: Fordham University Press, 2013).
Verene, Donald Phillip. *Hegel's Absolute: An Introduction to Reading the Phenomenology of Spirit* (Albany: State University New York Press, 2007).
Wachter, Susan M., and Kimberly A. Zeuli, eds. *Revitalizing American Cities* (Philadelphia: University of Pennsylvania Press, 2013).
Wade, Nicholas. "Scientists Seek Ban on Method of Editing the Human Genome," *New York Times*, March 20, 2015, A1.
Wall Street [Movie]. (1987).
Wallerstein, Immanuel. *World-Systems Analysis: An Introduction* (Durham, NC: Duke University Press, 2004).
Walzer, Michael. *Thinking Politically: Essays in Political Theory*, David Miller ed. (New Haven: Yale University Press, 2007.
Westerhoff, Jan. *Reality: A Very Short Introduction* (New York: Oxford University Press, 2012).
Williams, Alex "Robot-Proofing Your Child's Future," *New York Times*, December 14, 2017, D1.

Williams, Kevin D. "(R)Evolution of the Television Superhero: Comparing *Superfriends* and *Justice League* in Terms of Foreign Relations," *Journal of Popular Culture* 44, no. 6 (2011): 1333–1352.
Williams, Timothy. "For Shrinking Cities, Destruction Is a Path to Renewal," *New York Times*, November 12, 2013, A15.
Willse, Craig. *The Value of Homelessness: Managing Surplus Life in the United States* (Minneapolis: University of Minnesota Press, 2015).
Winters, Jeffrey A. *Oligarchy* (New York: Cambridge University Press, 2011).
Winters, Jeffrey A., and Benjamin I. Page. "Oligarchy in the United States," *Perspectives on Politics* 7, no. 4 (2009): 731–751.
Worland, Rick. "Captain Kirk: Cold Warrior," *Journal of Popular Film & Television* 16, no. 3 (1988): 109–117.
Worth, Robert F. "Aftershock," *New York Times Magazine*, June 12, 2016, MM28.
Zee, A. *Einstein Gravity in a Nutshell* (Princeton: Princeton University Press, 2013).

Index

"#TeamLucifer" (*Lucifer*) (2016), 51

"A Better World" (2003) (*Justice League*), 71, 72
"A No-Rough-Stuff-Type Deal" (2008) (*Breaking Bad*), 81
"A Piece of the Action" (1968) (*Star Trek* original series), 33, 43
Afghanistan War, 54, 69
"Alexander Kirk" (2016) (*The Blacklist*), 72
"All Goods Things . . . " (1994) (*Star Trek: The Next Generation*), 2, 61
"All Our Yesterdays" (1969) (*Star Trek* original series), 65
"Anomaly" (2003) (*Star Trek: Enterprise*), 70
"Arena" (1967) (*Star Trek* original series), 32, 43
"Author, Author" (2001) (*Star Trek: Voyager*), 78n26
"Awakening" (2004) (*Star Trek: Enterprise*), 47

"Balance of Terror" (1966) (*Star Trek* original series), 31

"Bar Association" (1996) (*Star Trek: Deep Space Nine*), 17n40
"Bread and Circuses" (1968) (*Star Trek* original series), 38
"Birthright" (1993) (*Star Trek: The Next Generation*), 45
Born on the 4th of July (1989), 52, 54
"Brothers" (1990) (*Star Trek: The Next Generation*), 66n8
"Bug" (2011) (*Breaking Bad*), 80
Bush George W., 38; Presidential administration (US) 54, 64, 68, 69, 70, 74

"Caballo sin Nombre" (2010) (*Breaking Bad*), 80
China, 5
"City on the Edge of Forever" (1967) (*Star Trek* original series), 35
"Cloud Minders" (1969) (*Star Trek* original series), 44, 76
Cold War, 13, 29, 30, 31, 32, 33, 35, 38, 39, 75
"Cornered" (2011) (*Breaking Bad*), 81

"Datalore" (1988) (*Star Trek: The Next Generation*), 66n8
"Day of the Dove" (1968) (*Star Trek* original series), 31, 43
"Dead Freight" (2012) (*Breaking Bad*), 81
Deerhunter (1978), 52

"Defiant" (1994) (*Star Trek: Deep Space Nine*), 73

"Encounter at Farpoint" (1987) (*Star Trek: The Next Generation*), 40n15, 66n4

"Errand of Mercy" (1967) (*Star Trek* original series), 30

"Extreme Measures" (1999) (*Star Trek: Deep Space Nine*), 78n21

"Face of the Enemy" (1993) (*Star Trek: The Next Generation*), 64

"Face Off" (2011) (*Breaking Bad*), 82

"False Profits" (1996) (*Star Trek: Voyager*), 9

"Fallen Hero" (2002) (*Star Trek: Enterprise*), 74

"Far Beyond the Stars" (1998) (*Star Trek: Deep Space Nine*), 43

"Farpoint Station" (1987) (*Star Trek: The Next Generation*), 56

"Felina" (2013) (*Breaking Bad*), 82

First Blood (1982), 52

"Friday's Child" (1967) (*Star Trek* original series), 36, 38, 43

"Future's End" (1996) (*Star Trek: Voyager*), 9, 85, 87

"Gina Zanetakos" (2013) (*The Blacklist*), 72

"Gray Matter" (2008) (*Breaking Bad*), 80

Green Zone (2010), 54

"Hazard Pay" (2012) (*Breaking Bad*), 80

"Heart of Glory" (1988) (*Star Trek: The Next Generation*), 60

Hegel, Georg, 1, 2, 6, 14, 23, 24, 60, 62, 66, 67, 76, 91, 92

"Homefront" (1996) (*Star Trek: Deep Space Nine*), 68

Hook, Sidney, 13–14

House of Cards, 75

"Improbable Cause" (1995) (*Star Trek: Deep Space Nine*), 73

"In the Cards" (1997) (*Star Trek: Deep Space Nine*), 11

"Inquisition" (1998) (*Star Trek: Deep Space Nine*), 78n20, 78n22

"Inter Arma Enim Silent Leges" (1999) (*Star Trek: Deep Space Nine*), 52, 75

Iraq (US Invasion of), 54, 64, 72, 74, 82

Johnson, Lyndon B. (US President), 75

Kennedy, John F. (US President), 75

"Kir'Shara" (2004) (*Star Trek: Enterprise*), 47

"Let That Be Your Last Battlefield" (1969) (*Star Trek* original series), 42

"Little Green Men" (1995) (*Star Trek: Deep Space Nine*), 17n31

Marx, Karl, 11, 12, 14, 51

"Measure of a Man" (1989) (*Star Trek: The Next Generation*), 60–61

"Memorial" (2000) (*Star Trek: Voyager*), 55, 56

"Mirror Mirror" (1967) (*Star Trek* original series), 37, 43, 75

Nazism, 29, 35, 39, 82

New York Times, 74

Nietzsche, Friedrich, 81, 82, 89, 93

No Escape (1994), 54

Obama, Barack (US President/administration of), 82

Of Men and War (2014), 51, 55

"Question Authority" (2005) (*Justice League Unlimited*), 70, 72, 73

"Quon Zhang" (2015) (*The Blacklist*), 74

"Paradise Lost" (1996) (*Star Trek: Deep Space Nine*), 53, 69

"Past Tense" (1995) (*Star Trek: Deep Space Nine*), 9, 46, 54

"Patterns of Force" (1968) (*Star Trek* original series), 33, 43, 82

"Pegasus" (1994) (*Star Trek: The Next Generation*), 53–54

"Phage" (1995) (*Star Trek: Voyager*), 85, 86

"Pilot" (*Breaking Bad*), 81

Polk, Sam, 8, 9

"Private Little War" (1968) (*Star Trek* original series), 32, 38, 43
Putin, Vladimir (Russian President), 75

Reagan, Ronald (US President), 5, 63
"Redemption" (1991) (*Star Trek: The Next Generation*), 53
"Reunion" (1990) (*Star Trek: The Next Generation*), 75
Russia, 5, 75

"Sacred Ground" (1996) (*Star Trek: Voyager*), 23
Schmitt, Carl, 63, 64, 68
"School of Hard Knocks" (2018) (*Blue Bloods*), 81
"Sarek" (1992) (*Star Trek: The Next Generation*), 53
Section 31, 72, 73, 74, 92
Soviet Union, 5, 63
"Space Seed" (1967) (*Star Trek* original series), 25n16, 90n14
Star Trek: First Contact (1996), 46, 64
Star Trek: Insurrection (1998), 53–54
Star Trek: Into Darkness (2013), 53–54, 73
"Susan Hargrave" (2016) (*The Blacklist*), 74

"The Apple" (1967) (*Star Trek* original series), 34, 35, 38, 65
"The Cloud Minders" (1969) (*Star Trek* original series), 44, 76
"The Dogs of War" (1999) (*Star Trek: Deep Space Nine*), 53
"The Doomsday Sanction" (2005) (*Justice League Unlimited*), 71, 73
"The Drumhead" (1991) (*Star Trek: The Next Generation*), 56
"The Expanse" (2003) (*Star Trek: Enterprise*), 68
"The First Duty" (1992) (*Star Trek: The Next Generation*), 53
"The Forge" (2004) (*Star Trek: Enterprise*), 47
"The Icarus Factor" (1989) (*Star Trek: The Next Generation*), 45
"The Killing Game" (1998) (*Star Trek: Voyager*), 83
The Man in the High Castle, 83

"The Measure of a Man" (1989) (*Star Trek: The Next Generation*), 60
"The Naked Now" (1987) (*Star Trek: The Next Generation*), 60
"The Neutral Zone" (1988) (*Star Trek: The Next Generation*), 9
"The Omega Glory" (1968) (*Star Trek* original series), 13, 31
"The Outrageous Okona" (1988) (*Star Trek: The Next Generation*), 62
"The Paradise Syndrome" (1968) (*Star Trek* original series), 36, 43
"The Savage Curtain" (1969) (*Star Trek* original series), 13, 27, 29
"The Schizoid Man" (1989) (*Star Trek: The Next Generation*), 62
"The Search" (1994) (*Star Trek: Deep Space Nine*), 52, 64
"The Shipment" (2003) (*Star Trek: Enterprise*), 49n18
"The Tholian Web" (1968) (*Star Trek* original series), 42
"The Ties That Bind" (2005) (*Justice League Unlimited*), 71
"The Void" (2001) (*Star Trek: Voyager*), 79, 84, 89, 93
"The Way of the Warrior" (1995) (*Star Trek: Deep Space Nine*), 53
"Think Tank" (1999) (*Star Trek: Voyager*), 85, 86
"This Side of Paradise" (1967) (*Star Trek* original series), 35
"To Another Shore" (2005) (*Justice League Unlimited*), 71
"To the Death" (1996) (*Star Trek: Deep Space Nine*), 64
"Transfigurations" (1990) (*Star Trek: The Next Generation*), 22
Trotsky, Leon, 11
Trump, Donald J., 3, 72, 75, 79, 82, 88, 89, 92
"Turnabout Intruder" (1969) (*Star Trek* original series), 62

Unitary Executive (theory of), 68
United States, 11, 13, 36, 69, 92

Wall Street (1987), 5

"When it Rains . . ." (1999) (*Star Trek: Deep Space Nine*), 75
"Who Watches the Watchers" (1989) (*Star Trek: The Next Generation*), 65

"Whom Gods Destroy" (1969) (*Star Trek* original series), 30

Zero Dark Thirty (2012), 69

About the Author

George A. Gonzalez (Ph.D., University of Southern California, 1997) is professor of political science at the University of Miami. He has been at the University of Miami since 1999. Gonzalez's area of research specialization is U.S. environmental politics and policy (e.g., energy, pollution, global warming). His books include *Energy and Empire: The Politics of Nuclear and Solar Power in the United States* (2012, State University of New York Press); *Energy and the Politics of the North Atlantic* (2013); *American Empire and the Canadian Oil Sands* (2016); as well as *Energy, the Modern State, and the American World System* (2018, State University of New York Press). Prof. Gonzalez has published research articles in *Polity* (the journal of the Northeastern Political Science Association). He has also published research articles in the journal of *Environmental Politics*, and in *Capitalism Nature Socialism*. In addition, Gonzalez has published original research in the journals of *Studies in American Political Development* and *Public Integrity*.

Professor Gonzalez also has a research agenda in the field of political theory and popular culture. In this area of study he has published articles in the journal *Foundation: The International Review of Science Fiction*, as well as the books *The Politics of Star Trek: Justice, War, and the Future* (2015); *The Absolute and Star Trek* (2017); *Star Trek and the Politics of Globalism* (2018); and *Popular Culture as Art and Knowledge: A Critique of Authoritarian Neoliberlism and the Crisis of Democracy* (2019). Primarily through the vehicle of the broadcast iterations of the Star Trek franchise, Gonzalez comments on metaphysics, international relations, justice, pragmatism, ethics, and the American left.

www.ingramcontent.com/pod-product-compliance
Lightning Source LLC
Chambersburg PA
CBHW020129010526
44115CB00008B/1034